So You Want

To Write A Book

❖

A Guidebook For Beginning Authors

Marshall Frank

Copyright © 2012 Marshall Frank

First edition

Cover design by Mia Crews (www.editorian.com)

ISBN-10: 0615706932

ISBN-13: 978-0615706931

Books by Marshall Frank

Beyond The Call

Dire Straits

Call Me Mommy

On My Father's Grave

The Latent: A Miami Novel

Frankly Speaking

Militant Islam in America

From Violins to Violence

Criminal InJustice in America

Messages: Short Stories for the Thoughtful

The Upside to Murder

So You Want to Write a Book

So You Want To Write A Book

ACKNOWLEDGEMENTS

I am one of those non-meticulous authors who transfer ideas from my head into words on a keyboard, looking up now and then to see if it is making any sense, and to count my typos. I could never have arrived at this point with a dozen published books without a perpetual shower of corrections and gotchas from readers, agents, critics and other authors. Thank you all, you know who you are.

Because this is a "How-To" guidebook for new authors, it needed fine tuning from a professional editor which is why I turned to my colleague, Celia Miles, of Asheville North Carolina, who did a superb (and embarrassing) job of making this right. See her web site at www.celiamiles.com.

Thanks also to Mia Crews and Karlene Conroy for their assistance in the formatting and final editing of this book. See their website at www.editorian.com.

Of course, no such accomplishment would ever be possible without the love and support of my best friend and partner for life, Suzanne, the most perfect human being on planet earth.

CONTENTS

PREFACE

This guidebook is for all those wannabe authors out there who have a book mulling around in their head and don't know what to do to get it rolling onto a manuscript. The greatest deterrent for most people is lack of confidence. Opening the door into the world of authoring is like passing into a dark hole. If you don't know where to turn or what lies ahead, the safest thing is to do nothing. The purpose of this guidebook is to turn on that light inside the dark hole so you can see what lies ahead and what's needed in the world of writing.

Can you write a book?

Anyone who can write can write a book. You don't need a soaring I.Q. or a career history in the war-torn Green Berets. There's nothing magical about the writing game; it's just another process to learn along with all its rules and tricks. All you need is genuine desire, a willingness to learn and a story to tell, whether truth or fiction.

I've heard people say, "I want to write a book, but who would care about my story?"

Start with your mom and dad, or your kids and their kids. Add your extended family and good friends. Before you know it, they tell other people and you've got a mailing list. You probably won't hit the best-seller charts on the *New York Times*, but so what? Your story is worthy to you and it will certainly be worthy to others. In modern times, anyone can have a book published, even if it's paid for.

Of course, some people are born with greater writing talents than others. That goes for all the arts, including music, painting and dance. While most people can draw a crude picture, some have more natural ability than others. Just because you're not a Rembrandt, does not mean you cannot paint a picture. I was born with an ability to play music by ear, yet I know graduates of

1

advanced music school and great musicians who cannot. They require a piece of written music before their eyes to play piano or violin. Who can explain it?

Anyone with average intelligence and an ability to write beyond text messages on a smart phone can write a short story or even a book. It's a matter of getting started with an objective, having a basic plan, making plenty of mistakes and learning from them. The key is to stay focused and determined.

I thought producing a book would be a simple task because writing came easy to me. In high school and college, I whizzed through written requirements, i.e., term papers, book reports and essays like a fish swimming through water. In the police department, I wrote investigative reports and administrative documents for thirty years. Other cops often asked me to do their reports for them. I suppose I was a natural.

After retiring from the police department, I entered the private sector working for a major security company. I had never read much fiction before, but now I wanted to know how to write a novel. My new job involved travel, which meant airports, airplanes, hotel rooms and restaurants, often alone. Plenty of dead time gave me a great opportunity for learning how to write novels by reading novels. I could carry the best classroom with me: Top authors and their books.

In those four years, I read over two hundred novels, studying the formation of plots and sub-plots, settings, character development, struggle, humor and tragedy. I saw how cleverly, yet simply, Sidney Sheldon crafted story lines and characters in his novels. I saw how John Grisham molded a legal story together with a key protagonist and a message buried in the novels. I saw that each author had their own style in crafting scenes, like parts of a movie. Mary Higgins Clark changed her chapters with every scene, Grisham blended two or three scenes into each chapter. Writing dialogue can be tricky, so I studied all the rights and wrongs, the rules, styles and tricks. I paid close attention to the use of italics, punctuation, flashbacks, prologues and epilogues, and so much more.

In 1995, shortly after full retirement, I first entered the dark hole with a story line. I wanted to tell about an old murder case where a group of white police officers beat an unarmed black motorist to death. They were later acquitted in court, leaving Miami, Florida, in the throes of the worst race riots in the history of the southeast United States. The media constantly attached "racism" as the core problem in the case, which incited the black populace. I had contended that racism actually played no role in this particular fiasco. It was manufactured by the sensation-thirsty media. I wanted to tell the real story from the inside, which I knew well. I had been the chief investigator.

A writer/mentor advised me that such a book should be fictionalized. She said I should tell the core story, but alter the settings and characters so no one is recognized. If I wrote non-fiction, I would identify many of the characters by name, leaving the door open for law suits by those who were portrayed less than flattering. That book ultimately became my first published novel, *Beyond the Call*.

It took me two years, revising and revising, writing and rewriting, to finish the first book without realizing it was actually a first draft. While I went about trying to secure an agent and/or publishers, I began working on a second book. Eventually, I landed a top New York agent who told me all the things that were wrong with the first book, which meant it had to be rewritten. It was too long, had too many words, too many sub-plots and was overly thick with descriptions and adjectives. *Beyond the Call* was originally 169,000 words.

I was determined to get it right. My agent strongly suggested that I lop off twelve chapters and 70,000 words to make it palatable for publication. That was an emotional trauma by itself, dumping so much good writing into the trash barrel.

In the interim, I finished another hard-boiled homicide thriller. *The Cocoplum Dilemma* was another good story about tough detectives and drug murders, much of it taken from true-life experience. That led to a dispute with my new agent who insisted I alter the story line with major changes, some of which I thought would ruin the suspense.

I reluctantly made most of the alterations he wanted, except for one. I was the rookie in this business, he was the old salt. But I stood my ground. One specific change was too drastic by my standards and not acceptable, so I invoked my prerogative as the author. It was a gamble.

I lost. Two weeks passed and the agent wrote me a curt letter telling me our relationship was over. I should find another agent. That was a hard lesson.

Now fifteen years and twelve published books later, I've learned many lessons, some the hard way. They afforded me mounds of knowledge I would never have acquired otherwise. They are lessons which I can pass on to other aspiring authors who simply don't know how to get started or finished.

That's the purpose of this book. To shed light on the unknown and to open that door without fear of what is on the other side, provide answers to questions and build confidence that you can do it.

You will also notice I cite several of my own novels and non-fiction books in various examples. They are the books I know most about, in which I made the most mistakes and later grew into the best of my writings. Yes, I am most definitely pitching the titles for anyone interested. A good author who cares about advancing his new career never stops promoting.

Meanwhile, as long as you stay grounded and keep your head in the real world without expecting million dollar contracts or movies from your book, you'll get the job done. It is highly satisfying to see your name on the spine of a book in a library or bookstore and to learn that someone who doesn't know you is willing to pay a few dollars to read your story.

Let's get started.

1

BEFORE STARTING

Preparation is everything. No one, experienced or not, simply sits down and pours out a book without first having a general idea of what they are writing about and why. New authors are often swamped with thoughts and ideas, but hesitate to begin because they are unsure of the mechanics, or lack confidence in their skills. Some don't even know why they want to write, they simply feel a compulsion, but don't know where or how to begin.

Hopefully, this chapter will offer some guidance in that regard.

ESTABLISH YOUR NEEDS AND GOALS

Why are you embarking on this writing project?

- You feel compelled to relate a specific story.
- You have many unusual life experiences to share.
- You love reading fiction and now you want to write fiction.
- It's the challenge. You want to see if you can do it.
- You have special knowledge or skills to pass on.
- You seek fame and riches.
- You're bored and need something to do.
- You want to see your book published.

Whatever your needs or your reasons, it's good to know what

you're getting into before you start. Be particularly realistic about getting published because there are numerous paths in that direction, some of which may be lucrative, but most are not. Getting an agent and a traditional publisher is not an easy task, but you can do it. We will address this subject more in detail in another chapter.

Writing a book consumes your time, it consumes your mind, your concentration and your energy. You will have to set other priorities aside in order to attend to your writing project. Forget about household repairs, forget about vacation, forget about playing golf. You will go to bed at night thinking about the book. You will wake up thinking about the book. Your spouse will catch you daydreaming at the table because you're mulling over a passage in the book. It is all-consuming.

Write when it's right for you. Some people have to get away to a remote location to dive into a writing project. Others hold full time jobs and set up their writing for a two-hour period every morning before work. It doesn't matter when you write or where, as long as you feel comfortable and can proceed without interruptions.

WRITING A SPECIFIC STORY

Perhaps something happened in your youth that turned life upside down: a train wreck; you were bullied, or victimized in some way. You experienced a war in which you, or a loved one, lost eyesight and two limbs. Perhaps a spouse was sent to prison for a crime he or she did not commit. You lived through riots, or a tsunami, or a deadly disease.

Event stories come in all sizes, eras, places and happenings. They can be told from a personal level or from the standpoint of detached knowledge. They are usually rife with emotion and/or excitement. You may want to share them with readers in non-fiction or fiction form.

It is up to you, the author, to decide how you want to tell the story, with real names and real happenings, or in fiction form using real people as models for your characters.

IMPARTING SPECIAL KNOWLEDGE

This category is unlimited, depending on the writer's background, experience, skills and education. Non-fiction informational books sell even better when the author is considered an "expert" in the genre. These books can deal with health, romance, automobiles, mechanics, real estate, finance, government, recipes, and anything else in human, or non-human, life experience.

Like most career police officers, I had a lot to say about the criminal justice system. Working within a major police agency in numerous assignments not only exposed me to the policing aspect, but to the entire justice system, from one end to the other.

I have strong ideas and opinions about the problems of crime in general, the so-called war on drugs, the issues of violence in the family, role modeling, sex crime, victimless crime, overcrowded prisons, overloaded courts, rehabilitation, and so forth. After all, I dealt with these issues first hand and saw what works and what doesn't work.

Politics and public image plays a major role in what laws are passed and enforced. If any politician came out and supported legal marijuana, he'd be assured of defeat at the polls after being labeled "soft on crime." It doesn't matter if it's a good idea, the public image matters more. These, and similar issues, are within my comfort zone of writing non-fiction.

In 2008 I unenthusiastically set out to pen *The Criminal InJustice System* because I needed to get all these feelings off my chest and move on. Blended with copious research and personal views, the book presents a myriad of alternatives to the current system that needed to be voiced by someone with my credentials. It was self-published because the topic is not of great interest to most people and no mainstream publisher would believe it could sell enough copies to be worth the investment. Nevertheless, it received great reviews and many readers have found it valuable. That's good enough for me.

In writing what you know, your skills and expertise will show through, and the reader will trust you. Even if you write about new recipes for baking cakes and pies, it can be of great interest to millions of people.

YOU WANT TO WRITE FICTION

Fiction lovers are often fiction writer wannabes. They have read so many wonderful novels about romance, mystery, sci-fi, children's stories, etc., they feel a heartbeat away from penning their own novel, complete with cast, plot, setting and all the elements necessary. It's a matter of forming a story and letting it flow through the fingers and onto the keyboard.

There are rules, written and unwritten, a fiction writer must follow if he or she expects to be published by a traditional publisher. More details on writing are coming further on in this guidebook.

YOU SEEK FAME AND RICHES

Good luck! Finding fame and wealth is a common dream; so is winning the lottery. We may all dream, but relatively few make it to the top. The key is to accept the outcome of your efforts without ever needing psychological therapy. You must be realistic. If you are really good, and you luck out, you can certainly make it rich.

I hope readers of this book will write the most successful book of the twenty-first century and make more money than J.K. Rowling and Stephen King combined. I believe in the American dream. I believe it may even come true for me one day, but I'm not holding my breath.

Disappointment comes with the territory. My dreams have been buoyed a number of times in the last fifteen years only to be shattered over and over. If you believe in yourself, never give up.

Twice, I have been represented by top agents in New York City. Twice, I have been dropped by those agents when the cards didn't play out very well.

Once, I was buoyed by a movie contract, with advance money and all. A producer sought me out after reading my novel, *Dire Straits*. I assisted in writing the screenplay. He thought it would make a great film, but in the long run he could not afford actor Andy Garcia as the main character, nor anyone else with star power. The movie was never made.

As I write this book today, someone in the film business in California is evaluating my novel, *Call Me Mommy*, for a screenplay. I'm grounded, still breathing normally. Expectations are low, while hopes are high.

There are certain realities that writers must know if they are counting on financial success:

1) One out of a thousand published authors makes enough money to eat.
2) You must have a good marketing plan and that often involves an agent and a publicist.
3) Getting published does not always equate to making much money.
4) Most major-league successful authors are published by large New York companies.
5) Have another source of income, besides authoring books. That is, if you want to keep eating.

YOU'RE BORED AND NEED SOMETHING TO DO

You want to climb the mountain because…well, it's there. You need a challenge. You want to see if you can do it. You want your dad, your spouse, your kids to be proud of you. Travel and golf are too expensive to take up all your down time in retirement, so you need a new activity. It will make you feel productive. You will leave a legacy of accomplishment outside of your career field. Your mind is constantly swimming with thoughts and ideas, and it's time to get them into writing. You want to confess your mistakes and boast about your accomplishments. You're a write-aholic, always at the computer churning out e-mails, letters to the editor, blogs and short stories. Now it's time to tackle a larger task: the book.

I once fantasized boarding an airplane – coach, of course – and sitting next to someone who was reading a book. It turned out to be mine. That's never happened. But I did find someone who had bought one of my used books at a library sale for fifty cents.

Oh well.

The dynamics of your personal life will dictate much of what you can do in the writing experience. A full time job and busy family life is not conducive to penning a book. The ideal American author is retired. An ex-cop, nurse, combat soldier, psychoanalyst, financier or a newly-freed mom pent up with thousands of experiences to share, with time available, can be a perfect candidate for pouring their energy onto the keyboard and then seeing it bloom into a book.

Even if you never make a lot of money, you will feel good about the sheer accomplishment.

Go for it.

EQUIPMENT NEEDS

This may sound elementary, but the generation who was not raised in the age of electronics need to know they cannot submit manuscripts created from a typewriter. That's like recording your music on a 78 rpm record.

Those days are gone, Grandpa.

The good news is that publishing companies don't even want you to send manuscripts in the mail any more. It's all done via computer attachments and/or flash drives that plug into computers.

Computers are everything. If you do not know how to use Word for Windows, Word Perfect or any other word processing program, I suggest you learn before getting started.

Word for Windows is the most popular and easiest for attaching entire documents to e-mails or onto flash drives and CDs. If you're going to write to get published you must have a good computer and all the associated equipment, such as printers and scanners, and must learn how to use them.

Word for Windows provides all kinds of writer aids, such as synonyms and language translations, bullets and more, but it is important to have a good dictionary and/or thesaurus handy for those touchy scenes where you want to capture the essence of your meaning. My favorite reference work is *Roget's International Thesaurus*. It offers a myriad of translations and nuances to your phrasing that can be an enormous aid in capturing the intent of your message.

Everyone has different styles and tastes. I'm a traditionalist who likes a desktop computer for extensive writing. Others prefer a laptop.

I know some writers who are stubborn and can (will) only

write with a pen and paper. That's fine if you have someone willing (or paid) to convert your hen scratchings into a computer generated document, and who can communicate and send documents via computer to agents and publishers.

Computers are non-negotiable. You won't get published without them.

Printers:

Make sure you have a laser printer, not an ink jet. Writing a book generates large documents. You will be printing anywhere from fifty to five hundred pages. Ink jet printers are notorious for guzzling ink, particularly the black color which is costly to keep replacing when the well runs dry. Toner can be expensive as well, but you will generally get around 2500 pages (or more) from one cartridge whereby you'll be lucky to get 500 pages from an ink cartridge.

It's simply more economical.

2

ELEVEN RULES FOR BEGINNING AUTHORS

1)   READ BOOKS

How could you learn to drive if you never rode in a car? How can you learn violin or piano if you never heard the sound of music? If you want to write a novel, read novels. If you are already reading novels, start re-reading your stories with a new and critical eye, not so much for the entertainment value, but the educational benefits. You can and should learn from other authors.

After deciding to write novels, I went about searching every major author of the day, particularly in mystery genre, plus some from bygone eras. Ernest Hemingway, Sidney Sheldon, Agatha Christie, Mickey Spillane, Anne Rice, Patricia Cornwell, John Grisham, Nicolas Sparks, James Patterson, Truman Capote, Joseph Wambaugh and others, have much to teach us about the writing game and how to structure a book.

Read! Read at least twenty different novels from different top level authors before you get started on your own.

For non-fiction writers, research topics that apply to your genre. Book stores and Amazon.com are replete with Do-It-Yourself manuals, cookbooks, diet books, political essays, biographies, history, travel and more. Read them, study them, pick out the styles you like best and emulate them. Some writers go into great detail; others skim over subjects. Some use a plethora of subtitles and subheadings; others do not.

Personal memoirs and autobiographies can be a little tricky, because they generally require writing in first person, i.e., "*I* grew up in Florida." '*I* loved *my* mother." "The problems were *mine*." The overuse of "me, myself and I" can eventually wear on the reader, so it's important to know how and when to refocus your images on other characters and/or events that impacted your life. Every president of the modern era has written his memoirs. So have most politicians and celebrities. They were usually assisted by professional writers and the structuring is generally very good.

My memoir, *From Violins to Violence,* received surprisingly rave reviews and was cited by a Melbourne, Florida, newspaper as the best book of the year 2007 by a local author. It follows my life growing up surrounded by mobsters, then entering a police career. It glosses over actual police cases and the personal struggles with family. It sold well. I consider it one of my best works, crafted and structured after other styles of more famous authors.

Photos in books is another matter that can inflate the cost of publishing. You should have an idea in advance of what kind of pictures you will include, and if they are in color or black & white. Learn by reading.

2) WRITE FOR THE PASSION

If you are writing a book for the money, don't go any further. It's the wrong reason.

Of course, every author hopes for great success and for the riches that come with fame. One must realize the odds are about the same as winning a lottery. Statistics on authors achieving financial success is dismal. Roughly one of every thousand published authors earned enough money from their books to eat. Most authors gross around four or five thousand dollars a year, less the cost of marketing and maintaining a personal inventory. If you can gross $25,000 a year, consider yourself a success.

Now and then authors do strike it rich. Their books will end up as movies, or they will catch the attention of top agents and publishers who will provide all the marketing they need. Repeat: That's one in a thousand authors.

The message here is to write for the love of writing. Write for the passion. Write to feel the breadth of your own accomplishment.

Write to send a message and hope you do better than expected. Money must be your secondary motive. Passion comes first.

3) CREATE A WRITING ENVIRONMENT

Writing a book requires intense concentration. Forget about your iPhone, forget about texting, forget about writing a few paragraphs between the innings of a ball game or your favorite TV show. You will need blocks of uninterrupted time and enough quiet so you are not distracted by television, conversation, or music.

The regimen varies with people according to their personal demands, quirks and habits. I wrote most of my early novels starting around 3 a.m. and working for six or seven straight hours a day. That worked best for me because there were no ringing phones or other demands on my time to distract and interrupt my thought process.

Other people work best in the evening and stay up late. Much may have to do with other members of your household and how you must adjust to their schedules. Most importantly you must have peace and quiet without disruption.

This is why older retired folks embark on book-writing projects more than younger people. For those with family between 25 and 55, and often in the prime of their career paths, it is nearly impossible to set time and location aside to concentrate on writing a book. Before starting on my first book, I was already in my mid-fifties and retired in the mountains of North Carolina. All my kids were grown and on their own.

There's another idea. Find a lonely island somewhere outside of Bali and set up shop for writing. Or Alaska. Or a mountain top in the Appalachian chain far from the big city. Do what works best for you, but avoid interruptions as much as possible.

4) KEEP AN OPEN MIND

If you are thin-skinned and have difficulty accepting criticism, find something else to do. Criticism is essential for new writers, and it is inevitable. Get used to it. And get over it. You will receive criticism whether you ask for it or not. It comes with the territory.

So maintain an open mind and welcome all the appraisals you can get, even the ones you don't like.

Critiquing is for all writers. Even the greatest of sports figures, musicians and artists continue relationships with coaches, teachers and mentors. Tiger Woods pays his coaches well despite being the greatest natural golfer of the last two decades. All opera divas continue lessons from their teachers. Writers need others to help guide and point out where they are going wrong. Critiquing is part of the writing mosaic if you are serious about finishing a book and getting it published.

Meanwhile, be open to exploring new ideas. Perhaps you have always written stories using third person narrative, but a writing coach suggests your new story should be in first person. Don't be so fast to decline. Experiment with the advice from another's perspective. Sometimes it works. Explore new ideas.

I've known new novelists who refused to listen to criticism; they were personally offended by being told there was something wrong with their writing, or their characters, or the setting. New writers tend to make mistakes, and corrections are part of the journey. Unless you want to go it alone, an easily damaged ego has no place in the writing experience.

5) BE HUMBLE

When you are the proverbial new kid on the block, listen more than talk. If you're lucky enough to have a writing mentor, share your thoughts and ideas, and show what you've written thus far. Prepare to do it over, to alter a scene, or a character, your phraseology, or simply to hear advice you didn't expect.

If your mentor is a skilled writer, listen carefully. If your mentor is an avid reader and not a writer, listen carefully. Readers are your bread and butter. They are the consumers, they know what turns them on and what does not.

Never get your feelings hurt. Overly sensitive new authors generally don't make it very far.

6) WRITE WHAT YOU KNOW

The last thing I would try to write about is sailing and fishing in the Pacific. Or the inner workings of diesel engines, or the intricacies of the stock market. On these subjects I am totally ignorant.

Tom Clancy writes military-based stories. He is not comfortable writing tearjerkers like Nicholas Sparks. Sparks is not an aficionado on military strategies and jargon. They each write what they know best. Attorney John Grisham's first eleven books featured lawyers as characters in plots about civil or criminal law. Only five of his twenty-eight books have deviated from the legal arena. The law is what he knows. Joseph Wambaugh, a former L.A. police detective, writes – you guessed it – police stories.

I write mostly about police investigations, the politics of running police agencies, music-based drama (I'm a trained violinist), some sports, troubled marriage, kids, drug abuse, murder, tragedy and community mayhem, because I have lived in those arenas.

Write what you know.

There are cooking recipes galore buried in our general populace that need to be unveiled. Potters and artists have an enormous reservoir of knowledge from which to teach others the art of molding clay and using a brush. Those who have traveled extensively abroad should think of sharing experiences in foreign lands. How do you quilt? How do you fix lawn mowers? How do you train a dog or a cat? What household remedies have improved your health?

Some people think they don't have an interesting enough background of interest to others. But they are usually wrong. It's not the subject matter that's lacking, it's the presentation. We all know others, among family, friends or co-workers, who have dealt with unusual struggles or lived through emotional trauma. There's always a story buried in there; writers just need to unearth the facts and present it in a pleasurable read.

7) RESEARCH WHAT YOU DON'T KNOW

If you plan to write a story that delves into areas you don't know much about, you must investigate and learn everything about that subject from the inside out. If you don't, ignorance will bleed through your writing and the reader will detect that you don't know what you're talking about. If you aren't up on a topic, don't try to wing it.

In the age of computers, anyone can be an investigator from the seat of a chair. It's easy to learn about other cultures, languages, technical information, history, politics and more with a single word: Google.

Nothing can be more embarrassing than a bona fide "Gotcha." Your friends and acquaintances will not hesitate to send you an e-mail saying, "George, nice book, but didn't you know that Riga is the capital city of Latvia, not Bulgaria?" Or, "You mixed present tense and past tense in the same sentence. Amateur!"

Whoops.

When you're writing about a small town in Missouri you've never seen, check it out thoroughly, call the Chamber of Commerce, read all the materials about it, even visit there if you can. I recently finished a novel where the protagonist had to fly his airplane to the Abaco Islands in the Bahamas. I've never been there, so I found someone who visited often and made lots of inquiries, plus I accessed all the political, cultural and geographical information I could find to make my scenes accurate.

Be correct. Investigate, probe, seek answers, delve into other worlds and learn. You'll be amazed at what you can uncover.

8) UNLEASH YOUR CREATIVE JUICES

Let the writing flow. You can tweak the text and make your corrections later. Don't re-read every sentence. Write paragraphs and chapters before checking them over.

For fiction, have a general story in mind you wish to tell. It needs characters, settings, flavors, smells, sounds, sights and most of all, feelings. Think about the basis for your story and how much you want to impart.

Don't worry about how silly it sounds, how poorly written it may be, or how discouraging the process. If you really want to write a novel, you can. You just have to want to, bad enough.

Explore your imagination. Include all kinds of emotions, fear, panic, sorrow, struggle, love, hate, revenge…and on and on. Add a little humor if you're so inclined. Carl Hiaasen is a Florida author who writes compelling dramas and mysteries, yet you'll go through some chapters laughing your head off. He has a unique talent. Maybe you do too.

9) REWRITE, REWRITE AND REWRITE

Be persistent. Don't give up. Be prepared for rejection and correction. The first draft is only a beginning. You will rewrite and rewrite, and rewrite again. It's all a part of the journey, especially for those just getting started.

Even if you are lucky enough to land an agent, he/she may have you make changes you didn't expect. Don't argue. You don't have the status of Stephen King who can dictate to his agents. You are only Mr. or Ms. McGoo, the wannabe author who needs to stop, look and listen, and eat humble pie if it means getting better and getting published.

Every sentence, every paragraph and every chapter will probably be rewritten to one degree or another. It's best you know that in advance.

10) BACK UP YOUR FILES

Can you imagine writing fifty pages of manuscript and suddenly your computer crashes and the hard drive is kaput? Everything is lost. You must start over from the beginning…that is, if you have the spirit to continue on.

Losing a single page or chapter can be devastating if you don't already have a printout or outline from which to restart.

Do not rely on electronics. Power outages and computer crashes can set you back days, weeks and months in a project. Always use a back-up system, whether it be CDs, flash drives or other downloads that will ensure everything you write is saved. And, save often.

11) GET STARTED

Start with the first word. Nothing happens when you stare at the keyboard.

3

GETTING PUBLISHED

Let's start off at the back end of the process.

Most new authors wonder first about what will happen after they complete their book project. How do I get published? How do I find an agent? What's self-publishing all about? What's the best way for me? These are questions you, the prospective author, are asking even before you write the first word.

Before getting into the mechanics of writing a book, we'll go over the basics.

PUBLISHING ROUTES

1) Do it yourself
2) Traditional publishing with a major publishing house
3) Acquiring an agent
4) Traditional publishing with a small press company
5) Traditional – Print-On-Demand
6) Self-published through an established company

DO IT YOURSELF

This is a literal term. It means to produce a book in a non-commercial manner, assembled in your office, garage or by a local printing/binding company. It won't have an ISBN or a bar code, it will never see a book shelf in Barnes & Noble and it probably will not be listed on Amazon.com, but, it will be *your* book. (ISBN stands for International Standard Book Number which is assigned to all books in the marketplace.)

A few years ago I spoke at a church assembly about the value of writing one's memoirs. After that talk, three members of the congregation, all seniors, set out to write their personal memoirs, complete with old photos, documents and genealogy records. They wanted to leave their life records to their great-grandchildren and their kids.

Two of those new authors did not bother to get published in a traditional book. Rather, they assembled writings, pictures and documents into a large three-ring notebook complete with dividers and tabs. *Voilà*, their memoirs were available to read by friends, family and great-grandchildren, and were quite interesting I might add.

I received an unsolicited book in the mail several years ago from a retired police colleague whom I had known for many decades. He had read my books and those of other ex-police officers and thought it was his time to share his thirty years of war stories and career experiences with friends and family. So, he finished the manuscript and called upon Office Depot for sizing and copying pages and having them bound into a spiral book. For a few dollars expense and his time assembling all the papers and pictures, his memoirs were available to read by friends and family. His book was interesting, indeed, especially to those who knew many of the characters and places in the writing.

None of these writers had any intention of selling their books. They only wanted to enjoy the feedback and to share their memories about interesting moments on the job, spiced with personal struggles and emotions to whatever degree they were willing to impart. Their books would also be treasured by ensuing generations of family members.

PUBLISHING COMPANIES - GENERAL

Money. Money. Money.

Set egos aside. The first thing you must know before dealing with publishing companies is that they don't really care about you or your book. They care about the potential profits. Publishing is a business, not a philanthropic endeavor. Publishers, editors and agents evaluate every submission based on its profit-making value. If they think they can make money on your book, the more likely they will publish it.

Even if they like your writing style or your subject matter, the bottom line is, "Will we make money on this book?" If it's doubtful, all the good writing in the world will not translate to getting published.

Another issue is marketability. What's hot? What's not? If St. Martin's Press has just released a few titles about mental telepathists solving murders, it's doubtful that the company will publish anything similar very soon after, no matter how good it is. One of my titles was rejected by two major houses with many compliments to the author. Reason: They had a glut on the market with police procedurals and didn't want to chance another release, back to back. When my agent called about the rejection, his words were, "The marketplace has spoken."

Self-publishing companies also expect to attain a certain level of profit income from the book before agreeing to publish, which usually entails investment by the authors themselves. There's a number of ways they can do this. Read on.

TRADITIONAL PUBLISHING – MAJOR COMPANY

Think in terms of Simon & Schuster, Doubleday, St. Martin's Press, Warner, Harper Collins, Random House – these are some of the big guns. The "major leagues," if you will. When you manage a book contract with one of them, you have arrived at an enviable level of success. That doesn't necessarily mean you'll make millions, but the chances are good that you will earn thousands.

These publishers are mostly based in or around New York City. They all carry enough clout to have books reviewed in advance by major newspapers and reputable reviewers that enhance sales. Their books all stand a better chance of being found on the shelves of Barnes & Noble or to see movie deals than any small press company. They all qualify for award submissions, including the Pulitzer. *Without exception*, they all require you to have a literary agent.

There's the rub.

You *must* acquire an agent before submitting to a major publisher. If you send your query or manuscript directly to one of the big guns, they won't open page one. They won't spend the time and trouble to mail it back. It will be as though you sent your manuscript to the planet Mars.

Publishing houses are inundated with thousands of submissions per year. Editors' desks are piled high with manuscripts and pleading letters telling of the magnificence of each and every author and their books. The editors need screeners. That's where the agents first come in.

Literary agents serve two purposes:

1) **Screening:** They are the threshold that major publishers rely upon for determining if the book is worthy of taking the time to evaluate. Publishers and editors usually establish a trusting relationship with certain agents of their liking. If the publishing company trusts the agent and he/she likes the book, you're in business.

Agents know the marketplace and what publishing companies are looking for and what they reject. If an agent suggests changes to your manuscript, it's for a reason. You may not like the editing process, but when you're the rookie in the field, you must listen to the old pros.

2) **Representing:** Agents act on your behalf to get a book into print. They are the go-between representing both sides, publisher and author. They will tell you what changes are needed, if any. They represent you like an attorney at contract time. They will take anywhere from ten to fifteen percent of your net sales as their fee for arranging your marketing events and dealing with the publishing company. They arrange reviews, they oversee reprints and movie deals. When you make money, they make money. That's the deal.

HOW TO ACQUIRE AN AGENT

Blind submissions do not work. If and when an agent receives an unsolicited manuscript, without first being queried, they will likely deposit it directly into the circular file. Forget about phone calls, e-mails and text messages. If you make contact with an agent that easily, there is something wrong. Either he or she is unsuccessful and hungry for any client, or they are fee-charging and make all their money from author wannabes. If that's the case, go the right way, even if it's the hard way.

Three common methods to attain an agent:

1) Query letters
2) Personal references
3) Writers conferences

Numerous sources exist for finding agents who represent your genre of book. *The Guide to Literary Agents,* published every year by Writer's Digest, contains a vast list of agent names and addresses, plus their specific genre preferences, i.e., Fiction or non-fiction only, Sci-Fi or mystery, Romance, Occult, Memoirs, Cook books. Most agents represent a full menu of genre, while some limit their representations to a more exclusive field, such as religious books or non-fiction only. A search on the Internet using Google: "Literary Agents" will result in a blast of sites from which to choose.

The listings will also provide agents specific submission requirements, such as "query letter only," or "two-page synopsis," or "send two chapters with bio." They do not all have the same requirements.

Rarely will they ask for attachments to e-mails, so be prepared to send a hard copy of your submission packed in a manuscript box via snail mail, along with a SASE (self addressed stamped envelope). Manuscripts should be sent via "media mail," which is about half the cost of regular mail. That requires a trip to the post office. You can send a manuscript via private postal services, like UPS or FedEx, but it's not likely to be read any sooner. Some agents may ask for a disc or flash drive with the document electronically copied.

It is important that you follow their precise instructions. This is an agent's first interaction with you and you want it to be positive. How you respond tells them what their future relationship with you might be like. Your letters, bios and synopses will give them insight into your writing skills.

Query letters

Query letters are the most common approach in the search for a literary agent. They should be one page, short, succinct and informational. Open the first paragraph with a quick bio, telling who you are and what makes you an authority on the subject matter. Do it in two sentences, if possible. Then sum up your book in two or three sentences. Avoid comments like "this is a great book" because they already know you feel that way. Tell them why it is a great book. What makes it unique? Why will it sell? And what types of people would bother to read (buy) it?

The query should also contain your credentials. Not an autobiography, not a Curriculum Vitae, just a couple sentences that explain your qualifications for writing this book, with educational degrees included. A sample query letter is in the back of this guidebook.

A synopsis, if requested, should be limited to two or three pages, telling a little more about the story and its characters. Don't hesitate to reveal the ending if you think it's pertinent to selling the book. The agent is a business person evaluating its potential, not an average reader you want to surprise at the end. Writing synopses is a true test of writing talent. A synopsis must say much in a few words. A sample synopsis is in the back of this guidebook.

Include your author bio in every submission on a separate page. One or two short paragraphs will do. Emphasize your education and/or experience in the genre you're writing about. A sample bio is in the back of this guidebook.

Remember, when agents see a massive block of words on your letter and associated materials, they will be less inclined to read it. Keep it tight and to the point. If you make a good impression, they will ask for more at a later time.

Personal References

If you are lucky enough to know a published author or other

person who has contacts in the publishing world, and they like your material, they might refer you to an agent, whether their own or someone they know. Agents will listen to Mary Higgins Clark or James Patterson if they say you've got the right stuff.

I acquired my first agent from a referral from an established author. I thought I hit the big time. The agent liked my writing but – as I pointed out earlier – he suggested some changes. I did not make those changes and he dropped me like the proverbial hot potato.

It was my fault.

Writers Conferences

You can acquire agents by attending writers conferences, either in your communities or other major population centers. These conferences usually offer several workshops and mini-seminars, speakers, "meet and greet" events and interaction with invited agents who are there to review a few pages of manuscripts for a small fee.

You can find scheduled conferences on line or through your local writers organizations. Every medium and large sized community in America has writers organizations where writers of all types meet periodically for interaction, social events, informational meetings and critique groups. These groups will know where the nearest conferences are being held. Some hold conferences of their own.

Maybe one out of every twenty wannabe authors will end up with a contract with an agent from one of these conferences. Those are better odds than blind query letters because the agents get to meet you personally. It works like this:

You sign up for the conference, which usually costs anywhere from $75 to $275. You apply for a meeting with an agent, which requires you to send a few pages of your manuscript plus a synopsis. That also requires an extra fee. At the conferences, you will be scheduled with an agent who has read your submission and will spend from five to twenty minutes with you for a critique of your work. If the agent sees good writing and marketing potential, you might come away with a contract.

I've known several authors who attended conferences in

Atlanta, Orlando and Miami where they acquired agents. It's doable. You have to be confident and tenacious, and your manuscript must be in finished condition, ready for professional review.

A note of caution: Read the fine print. Beware of fee charging agents. Many agents make their money from reading fees paid by aspiring authors. While authors hope and pray for representation, that's a rarity among fee chargers because that's the way they make money. Publishing companies also know who the fee charging agents are. Publishers are less likely to deal with them than standard agents who only make their money when the authors make their money.

TRADITIONAL PUBLISHER – SMALL PRESS

Small press translates to getting your book into the marketplace by a respectable publisher, but without expectations of making a lot of money. Small press publishers can be likened to the "minor leagues."

When *Dire Straits* was rejected by major league publishers, my agent suggested I submit to smaller publishing companies. There are plenty of those. After a dozen submissions and queries, I found Harlan Publishing in North Carolina that specialized in hard-boiled cop stories, my genre. I made it in the minor leagues and that was okay with me.

One difference in submitting to a minor league publisher is that you do not always need an agent. Many small press companies will accept your queries directly and respond directly. The Internet can provide you with a wide array of small press publishing companies and their preferences for genre and submission guidelines. Those listings will tell you whether they require an agent or not.

Depending on the size and success of the company, small press publishers generally will not print more than 3,000 copies of a book once it is released. It will be available through the traditional market sources, usually via a distributor. The most commonly used distributors are Ingram or Baker & Taylor. Retail stores generally order their books from distributors.

Well established small press companies will list their books as "returnable," which means they can be ordered by a retail book store such as Barnes & Noble, and the stores can return any unsold books to the publisher for wholesale compensation. This is particularly important for author book signings. Retail stores do not warehouse books unless it's very likely they will be sold. If you're not famous or you do not have a listing with the *NY Times*, it's not likely that the store will keep your books on the shelf. Most books that are not sold at signings will be shipped back to the publisher.

A good source for finding small publishers is in local or state listings. Many publishers are state-based, preferring to promote local authors and/or stories set in local venues. Pineapple Press, based in Sarasota, Florida publishes only stories and non-fiction books which are set in Florida. The Florida Historical Society is very open to publishing fiction and non-fiction that encompasses some element of Florida history. There are similar publishers in every state in the union.

PRINT-ON-DEMAND (POD)

These are small press companies who operate much the same as other publishers, with major exceptions. First, they do not warehouse books. Second, books are printed only when an order is received. Third, books are *not* returnable to the publisher if unsold.

Retail book stores will seldom order books from distributors or publishers that are not returnable. That usually scuttles an author's chance for book signings at a retail site.

However, independently owned bookstores, not beholden to a mega chain with a central corporate policy, can do as they choose. If you have a following in your community and the book store is ready to support you by ordering non-returnable books, that means they feel there is a good chance the books will be sold from the shelf. Some authors develop a special relationship with book store managers in their towns and cities.

Independent book stores may also agree to order books for a signing if you, the author, agree to buy back the unsold books at their cost.

Companies like Aberdeen Bay Press and Publish America, who have published my work, may bear the cost of publishing your books and market the title through the normal systems and distributors, including Amazon.com. But the chance of getting your book into a signing at Barnes & Noble is almost nil.

These companies rely on the author to help with sales and marketing, which means they will want their authors to purchase a number of books for their own inventory. When I published *The Upside to Murder* through Aberdeen Bay Press, I agreed to buy two hundred books to start, then more when that supply was depleted. That assured the company they were not going to take a loss and they would be selling more books through the online systems.

Other companies make their money by attaching a high retail price to the book, then sell authors the books at a thirty percent discount from retail. Thus, your book may be listed at $25, and you must pay $17.50 each for your own copies, a hefty price. Depending on the word count, the printing cost to the publisher for an average book is around three to four dollars, when many are ordered in bulk. That's a profit for the publisher, even if you only buy one hundred books. Books by unknown authors that list for $25 are not likely to fly off the shelf.

Each company has its own policies and rules. The bottom line is they are all in business to make money, not lose money.

SELF-PUBLISHING

Simply put, this is when authors pay a company to publish their books.

Two-thirds of all books are published by this method today. Self-publishing has become the easiest and most popular route for new authors to see their books in print. Years ago, it was called "Vanity Press," which connoted an amateur writer whereby most people looked down their noses at the product of such authors.

That's no longer the case.

With print-on-demand systems emerging in the modern computer era and the absence of warehousing needs, self-publishing and POD companies have risen to prominence all over America. All it takes to get published is money (a set-up fee), or the author buying a minimum number of books, plus following the companies guidelines and standards. Some self-publishing houses will not accept explicit sexual material or anti-religious text. Some limit their publications to gay/lesbian themes. Each company posts its guidelines in a clear manner.

These companies are legitimate publishing companies that produce a professional product with book cover designs, ISBNs and bar codes. They market your books on the Amazon.com and Barnes & Noble websites, use Ingram distributors and deal with book stores that ask for them. Because it is so tough to get published by traditional publishers today, many capable authors turn to self-publishing to get their book into print.

Some self-published books are unprofessionally written because the threshold for getting published is much less stringent than traditional publishers. Some of the self-publishing companies don't care how well the book is written; they care about the money you pay and the number of books you, the author, will buy for your own inventory.

Regardless, there are fabulous books that have won awards and sold thousands or millions of copies that originated as a POD or self-published book. As I write this guidebook, the best-selling book on charts all over the world is *Fifty Shades of Grey,* by E.L. James, published as a POD paperback in 2011 by The Writer's Coffee Workshop, based in Australia. Now, it's a best seller around the world exceeding J.K. Rowling, the author of the Harry Potter series. It has soared to the top of the publishing field with two sequels and is certain to be made into a motion picture. The book, which is mired in erotica, was picked up by an imprint of Random House not long after it made a huge splash in the marketplace. The author is raking in millions.

Writer/lawyer Deborah L. Jacobs self-published her book, *Estate Planning Smarts,* and embarked upon a robust marketing plan that drew the attention of a major publisher. Now she's on the Best Seller list. She wrote a superb article about her success in *Forbes Magazine* titled, *"How My book Became a Best Seller."*

John Kremer's, *Self-Publishing Hall of Fame*, lists hundreds of self-published authors who have gone on to great success.

With two of my books, I knew the chances of high sales were unlikely, but I wanted to get the books into print. My non-fiction opus, *Criminal InJustice in America,* had been a goal since I retired from law enforcement. With thirty years of background watching the justice system struggle in quicksand, I wanted to convey my thoughts and knowledge about cops, courts, prisons, justice and all that is wrong with the failed system into a book for public exposure. I also knew that criminal justice is not a high priority topic with readers in general. The chance for a traditional publisher risking time and money on a losing proposition was slim to none. I went to Author House, a reputable self-publishing company to handle my book. I paid less than one thousand dollars for them to do the cover and the associated publishing requirements. From there, I bought a significant number of books for my inventory at approximately half the retail cost. I have been satisfied with the results.

Did I make money? Yes.

Enough to support me and my family? No.

I also paid Author House to publish *Messages: Short Stories for the Thoughtful,* another book that I knew would never be a big seller. This 158-page edition contains a variety of short stories that I had written over fifteen years and kept stored away in my hard drive never knowing what I would do with them. Someone suggested I should assemble them into one book. So, I did.

These two books are not hot sellers, but they do make great gifts or sales bonuses with other books when offering a discount at author's cost. I sometimes use these books as prizes for the audience when performing music gigs and seminars.

With self-publishing, as with POD, all the marketing is entirely up to you, the author. The publishing company has already made its money. Do not expect your self-published book to be on the shelf of retail book stores. It's not going to happen. Book stores have gone out of business in recent years because the demand for hard copy is declining in the electronic age. Borders is gone, along with Waldenbooks, B. Daltons and many independents. Your income from self-publishing depends on you, your time, your ingenuity and your energy. You must buy books for inventory, you need a mailing list, you need to arrange book talks and signings and anything else you can do to sell. If you don't market, that's your choice. It's your money.

We'll talk more about marketing later on in this book.

THE EDITING PROCESS

Get it right. Don't settle for mediocre.

Whether you're dealing with a mega publisher like Random House or a small Podunk self-publishing company, here's the best advice anyone can give: Get your manuscript professionally edited before you submit it.

For self-published and POD authors, nothing is more embarrassing and damaging to a reputation than to produce a book replete with errors in syntax, spelling, punctuation, dialogue, poor sentence construction, overused adjectives, underdeveloped plot and characters, and overused subplots. The book may have had potential, but if it appears amateurish, readers will not recommend it to others, and poor reviews will follow. That's a death knell to your future as an author.

Mistakes stand out like a huge boil on the tip of the nose.

Standard publishing companies do not edit any more. Not much, anyway. They expect your book to be submitted in pristine shape, fine-tuned before it ever reaches their desks. Agents do not edit either, but if they think your book has sales potential they will either recommend a good editor or provide some of their own tips.

You cannot rely on your grandma, brother, mother or best friend to edit your book, no matter how educated or skilled they are as readers or writers. They are too close to you to be impartial, they will couch criticism to avoid hurt feelings, and they will not have a full understanding of all the necessities that go into preparing a finished manuscript. There's much more to editing than punctuation.

Good editors can be very expensive, but some are not. At the very least, be prepared to spend $2.50 a page (or more), double-spaced, for editing a full manuscript. For a three-hundred page manuscript, that would cost you $750. That's not bad. Top professionals can charge thousands for the same size manuscript. When you become an experienced author and have established relationships with editors through networking, you may work out deals that are very reasonable.

Another less expensive source for editing assistance is from critique groups, peer writers and authors who meet at designated times and venues to discuss each other's work in progress. More on this valuable resource is discussed in Chapter Seven, under the subheading Critique Groups.

4

WRITING NOVELS

"It ain't as easy as it looks."
- Anonymous

Delving into fiction means knowing how a novel is crafted. You cannot know that unless you have read novels, thus the first "Rule" in Chapter Two: *Read Books*.

Fiction writing requires a fluid mind and a vivid imagination. It's like being a kid playing "let's pretend," making up story details as you go. You create scenes the same as a director creates scenes in a movie. They all come alive with characters, places, props, sounds, feelings, struggles, laughter, love, hate and, most of all, a purpose. It is essential that you have a central theme and a protagonist, a main character that drives the story. The number of secondary characters depends on the story itself. Some stories have multiple sub-plots and many characters that interweave. They present a challenge to the author to keep the flow moving and the reader interested in the story.

Ernest Hemingway's classic novel, *The Old Man and The Sea*, featured a single character about a man struggling to survive in the ocean with a huge catch, reflecting on his personal life and background along the way.

Ask yourself what you hope for readers to get out of your story.

1) **Anticipation:** You want your reader to anticipate every scene, to wonder *What's happening next?*

2) **Information:** As you tell a story, you also want to be a teacher. You want readers to end your book feeling they have learned something they never knew before. You can write about police work, military experiences, hospital emergency rooms, piloting jets, diving in the ocean depths, life in Amish communities or Islamic countries and hundreds of other topics that most people know little about.

3) **Emotions:** Most of all, you want to stimulate the reader's emotions. The more emotion you stir, the more readers will admire the writing. Nicholas Sparks writes smaller books than most novelists, but his emotional output is so powerful, he leaves the reader in tears. Carl Hiaasen provides suspense, but he also makes you laugh. James Michener takes you around the world into the depths of other cultures. Stephen King has you on the edge of your seat with chills and fear, aghast at what some humans will do to other humans.

Set a goal you want to accomplish in telling your story. You can deviate from that along the way as you see fit, but a general goal will keep you on track. Write your first couple of chapters before rewriting anything. Have someone (an experienced reader) look over your first efforts and give you feedback.

Most importantly, don't give up. Write a book. You *can* do it. All you need is the desire and determination.

MANAGING YOUR OUTLINE

There is no perfect prescription for the regimen and personal organization for writing a novel. Writers have their individual styles, habits and idiosyncrasies.

Some authors are extremely organized. They feel compelled to create a detailed outline of the entire book with short summaries of every chapter before writing the first word of Chapter One. They are perfectionist fusspots, but they often write great books. Some write brief preliminary biographies of their fictional characters as though they actually existed. It helps to guide them through the story.

Other writers, like me, shoot more from the hip; pondering a plot, inventing a few characters, and then sitting down to let the fingers fly while the mind flows into fantasyland. I make up scenes as I go along, while adhering to the basic story line. My ideas come when I'm driving a car, walking in the park, sitting at restaurants ignoring a dull conversation, watching a movie scene that triggers a reminder, reading a newspaper, lying in bed before rising early in the morning or listening to an engaging story about someone else. Once you get rolling on a writing project, you never know when a great thought will rise to the surface of the brain.

Some writers must get away to a lonely island or a mountain top and dedicate their life to completing the book. Others can go about their daily lives and set aside a couple hours a day in the morning or the evening. It all depends on your personal and business demands. If you are retired, all the better; time is at your beck and call to manage as you wish.

Do what works best for you.

GENRE

The book market is divided into many genres, one of which should fit your novel, because that's where your book will be pigeonholed in every website, every book store and every book fair. While your story may include love and romance, high-tech military operations and murder mystery all in one, you'll be required to identify it with one predominant genre.

My novels are generally categorized as mystery although some of them are not so much mystery, but suspense thrillers and police procedurals balled into one. For the purpose of marketing, I choose the "mystery" label because it is the most popular of the police-related genres, and it's appropriate.

In two of my books, the mystery is not so much about who committed the crime, but how the killer(s) would ever get caught and/or how the police could solve the crime.

So, it's up to you. Select a genre that is right for your book.

According to a number of combined sources, here are the three most popular genres in fiction:

- Mystery/Thriller/Crime - nearly 40% of the fiction market
- Science Fiction - about 25% of the fiction market
- Romance - about 20% of the market

Other genres for fiction to consider are:

- Western
- Historical
- Inspirational (religious)
- Political
- Fantasy
- Gay & Lesbian
- Military/War
- Sports

There are more, but you get the point. Not to be overlooked and very popular in fiction, are books for children and young adults. These can be written as fantasy, inspirational and other genres, but they are – for the most part – devoid of extreme violence, sexual content and bad language. The protagonist and supporting characters are usually children, teens and/or animals.

Bear in mind that children's fiction usually requires illustrations and/or photographs. The more pictures you need, particularly color, the more cost in producing the book. Many children's authors seek the collaboration of an artist to illustrate their books, with a predetermined deal as a lump sum, or a percentage of the income. It is not uncommon to find children's books written by the illustrators. Such a deal.

TRANSPOSING TRUTH INTO FICTION

Are you trying to tell a true story of which you have intimate knowledge? Perhaps you were closely involved in a case of child neglect, suffered an abusive relationship, subjected to improper or illegal treatment on the job, and you want to tell the story through fictional characters. Perhaps you know someone else who shared their personal horror story with you. Here are a few guidelines for converting true events and real people into a novel.

When you fictionalize a true story, you have a literary license to stray from the hard facts about characters, plot and setting. You can add or subtract fictional nuances and events that provide more excitement and/or interest to the reader. In other words, you make up scenes, characters and dialogue to add color to the novel, but adhere to the core story and the primary message. This also tests your creativity.

I knew one writer who had extreme difficulty writing a true story into fiction because she felt she had to stick firmly to the exact details of the events. She got mired into minutia, unable to move on from one chapter to another, worried that she didn't record the facts exactly as they happened. Precise recording is not necessary when you are writing fiction. After all, who is going to know the difference? You can always employ literary license, and no one will know what details have been removed, added or altered. If accuracy is that important, consider changing to non-fiction.

In writing fiction based on truth, you must be aware of the risk of liability if one or more persons (who are living) claim you identified him/her in an offensive or inaccurate manner. Using a pseudonym for a character is not always sufficient. You may think you cannot be held liable for defamation of character, but that's not always true. If someone claims your disreputable character is close to him or her in appearance, personality, background or deeds and can be readily identified by readers who know that person, you can be sued. Of course, the plaintiff must be able to show how and why he/she was damaged in some way, or the suit won't go very far (i.e., lost job, lost money, lost reputation).

I have had two personal experiences in both these kinds of situations.

In *Beyond the Call*, my goal was to tell the true story behind the killing of an unarmed black man who was chased by a dozen angry police officers. When finally apprehended, the cops beat him to death. The media and the community were up in arms claiming this was a racist-based crime, and demanded retribution disguised as justice. Five officers eventually charged and tried for the crime, were all acquitted. That verdict triggered the Miami Liberty City riots of May, 1980, in which eighteen innocent people were murdered.

The department was much to blame for not properly dealing with a few rogue officers over the years when they had exhibited violent tendencies. That was the story I wanted to tell. In doing so, I altered some of the facts but stuck to the core issue:

- I changed the setting from Liberty City to the rural area of Dade County.
- I changed the vehicle being chased from a motorcycle to a Chevy Nova.
- I changed the victim from a black man to a white man, thereby removing the racial element from controversy.
- Besides name changes, I altered the physical appearances and ethnicity of the rogue cops, from fat to skinny, tall to short, Italian to Polish, and so forth.
- I created a protagonist (primary character) to drive the story from beginning to end, seeing the events unfold from the point of view of a rookie cop who was assigned to the rogue officers for training. In fact, that character did not exist in real life.

Call Me Mommy mirrored a true story about a child from a broken home who was torn between a good mother and contemptible father who, unfortunately for the child, had been awarded custody. The story contained some vile characters along the way, including one slovenly woman of low moral character. The description of that character was ultimately read by a woman (formerly part of my extended family) who claimed the character was her in real life. She sued me for defamation. She didn't win, but I still paid a healthy fee for a defense attorney to represent me.

In truth, I had made the character too similar.

ELICITING EMOTIONAL RESPONSES

Emotions are what readers are looking for.

Mystery writers should strive to provoke readers into wanting to learn more and more about a person, place or event. Good thrillers are rife with anticipation whereby people can't wait to turn the pages. Romance fiction must draw pangs of love and desire. Children who are suffering abuse, neglect, injury and disease pull at the heart strings. As a writer, you want readers to be emotionally involved as though they are in those very scenes watching and listening and feeling as the story plays out. You want readers to feel what they are feeling in a movie, how Humphrey Bogart and Ingrid Bergman felt in *Casablanca*, or the pain of Meryl Streep in *Sophie's Choice,* and the emotional conflicts of Kate Winslet in *Titanic.*

Emotional responses from the reader are based on two factors:

1) A compelling story line – and/or
2) A compelling character or set of characters.

Here you need good pre-readers and a good editor. A critique group with skilled authors can give feedback about the power, or lack of power, in your story. If you respect the writers in your group, pay close attention to what they tell you. A good editor will not only correct syntax and punctuation, he/she will provide feedback about plot, intensity, pace and other factors that improve the book.

THE OPENING SCENE

Start with a hook. Grab the reader in your beginning chapter, your beginning scene or your beginning sentences. Make the reader wonder about what's to come in the following pages.

One common technique is to begin a novel by titillating the reader with a compelling scene from the middle of the book. After starting the next chapter at the beginning of the story, the reader will already be instilled with anticipation wondering how the story leads to that scene.

In *The Upside to Murder,* the opening scene is a quiet day on a Florida beach where a little boy pees on the edge of the surf and watches a red sneaker floating in on a wave. Curiously, he investigates the strange object and finds a rotting human foot inside being eaten by crabs. Mommy and Daddy call the police. It takes twenty chapters in the book to learn how and why that discovery is of significance to the murder case upon which the story is based.

On My Father's Grave begins in 1959 when a symphony musician is walking alone from a concert on a darkened New York City sidewalk. He's kidnapped at gunpoint and delivered to a Mafioso mobster. This sets the stage for a story about a woman in 2003 who embarks on a search of a long lost father she never knew.

Some novels start with very violent or emotional scenes. That usually grabs the reader into wondering who did it, why it was done, who investigates, what methods are used and what obstacles everyone must cross. It piques interest.

The story must move along and maintain a pace. Something must be happening in every scene. If the book starts out boring for the first three chapters, you'll lose the reader. Be sure to end most chapters with a "hook," a line or two that entices the reader to open the next scene.

Suddenly, a knock came at the door.
When she saw the driver stopped at the red light, she nearly passed out.
Macbride thought he had his man. Little did he know.

Most important to a novel is your main character (protagonist) and the supporting characters. Your primary character should be someone who is cared about, who elicits a special feeling. He/she should be likeable, sympathetic, dynamic, interesting, suffering, troubled, innocent, and sometimes even guilty. Yes, readers can develop a kinship to the bad guy. In my most recent release, *The Upside to Murder*, the primary character commits two cold-blooded murders, yet readers root for him throughout the entire story.

The reader's emotions should be formed into caring for the protagonist, wanting to know what will happen to him/her. In many books, supporting characters also become important to the reader, including the contemptible, criminals and abusers.

THE NOVELIST AS A TEACHER

Readers want to be entertained and amused, but they love to finish a book feeling enlightened, thinking they learned things they didn't know before.

In *Beyond the Call*, I wanted readers to learn what happens inside the bowels of a police agency when middle-range supervisors either ignore or protect bad behavior among police officers who are abusive, dishonest and corrupt. I needed to show it was not only the brutal acts of rogue cops that resulted in the killing of an unarmed motorcyclist, but blame also lay with the department's higher echelon who should have seen it coming.

Call Me Mommy, my intent was to teach the reader about the influence that an incompetent or deranged parent can have on the development of a growing child. I wanted to identify the roots of drug addiction and the miserable lifestyle that often follows. I wanted to enlighten people about the problems of enabling, and all the heartbreaks that evolve from dealing with an addict in the family.

Tom Clancy's novels teach us all about military process and technology. John Grisham familiarizes us with the hurdles of the justice system, both civil and criminal. Stephen King and J. K. Rowling teach us about fantasy and the power of imagination.

You may want to write a religious novel teaching the reader about the power of God and/or Jesus to a person who has gone astray. Your story may bring readers to other lands you know so well, and when the book is finished, they will feel like they've been to Bangladesh, Madagascar, Mecca or Prague. If your story is based in rural America, (providing it fits within the scene of the story) you may want to share your grandmother's recipe for pecan pie, or the methods for whittling wood into a musical dulcimer.

The key is to not over teach. Don't lead your reader by the nose. Let your story and your characters do the teaching through dialogue and circumstance. Gary Provost, a great writer/teacher, often said, "Show, don't tell." Think of someone verbally droning about computer technology instead of sitting down and showing you, hands on. Think about someone talking your ear off describing the yacht basin, versus taking you there in person. Bring your readers into the setting. Show them what happens. Trust them to learn what you intended.

GETTING TECHNICAL

Be careful. Novel readers are interested in being moved and entertained. They are not usually interested in high-tech, scientific minutia that bores the average human being. They want story, motion, emotions, human experience and suspense of some kind.

There are exceptions. Military officers and munitions experts love Tom Clancy because they can relate to the government/ military genre he presents with such clarity. Author Lee Boyland familiarizes us with high-tech nuclear physics and as it relates to weaponry in his trilogy, starting with *Rings Of Allah*. He also teaches about the problems of radical Islam in the global front. Authors of the twenty-first century rely greatly on computer technology in forming their story, but they must be careful not to venture out of the realm of comprehension. When readers don't comprehend, they become impatient and put the book aside.

Remember, novels are primarily intended to entertain or evoke emotion. Never lose sight of that.

COMPONENTS OF A NOVEL

With some variations, most novels consist of the following elements:

- The title
- Characterization
- Names for characters
- Dialogue
- Point of view
- Past or present tense
- Setting
- Plot
- Chapters
- Human senses

Choosing a Title

The title is up to the author, but don't be surprised if a publisher or agent convinces you to make a change. In many cases, these suggestions are relevant to non-fiction books as well.

The best titles are short and mysterious. Wordy titles tell too much of a story and may sound amateurish. *The Day Mary Went to a Wedding Reception Gone Wrong.* Shorten that to: *The Wedding Reception.*

There are two titles an author can assign their books. The first is created during the writing phase, denoted in a Word (computer) file for easy access, as a "working title." Working titles are often changed into a final title when the book is finished, after much fodder is provided in the text itself. An author may want to use a single line from dialogue for the title, as I did in *On My Father's Grave.* In it, a distraught adult daughter of a missing father for forty years courageously confronts an old Mafioso fellow who knows all the answers to her mystery. When she thinks he is lying and demands more of the truth, he responds, "I swear, on my father's grave." Thus, the title. Before that, the working title was *Finding Father.*

Beyond The Call was paraphrased from a character's comment about the way a group of cops went into a frenzy beating a man to death.

My novel, *Dire Straits,* was originally titled *The Cocoplum Dilemma,* but changed at the insistence of an agent. Cocoplum is an upscale neighborhood in Miami, Florida where a mass drug-related murder takes place in the story. My agent suggested I change that title because the term "Cocoplum" was unfamiliar to readers outside Miami. I responded, "But no one knew what Andromeda meant in Crichton's *The Andromeda Strain.*"

He answered, "You're not Michael Crichton."

Touché. I changed it to *Dire Straits.*

John Grisham's genius is shown is many of his titles which draw readers with a single word: *The Client, The Witness, The Firm, The Rainmaker* and so forth.

My fifth novel, *The Latent,* is about a murder case which yields a single palm print from the taut skin of the victim. It is later identified to the least suspicious person. Only a single word is needed.

If and when you are stumped, go to a book store and study the titles in your specific genre, and ideas will come. A title is very important. It is meant to create curiosity in prospective readers. It should be relevant, mysterious and subtle.

Regardless, this is **your** book, your creation. Title it as **you** deem appropriate.

Characterization

The story begins and ends with the life experience of one or more human beings. You must have a main character, a protagonist, who propels the basic story line. Of course, the book will likely have other supporting characters, some more important than others. You must present a person with whom the reader will become engrossed, whom the reader will care about, and for whom the reader develops a degree of fascination. The primary character is the wind beneath the wings of a gripping plot. (How's that for a new metaphor?)

While it is important that a reader develop a physical image of the character, you must avoid over-describing from the omniscient narrator. That's you, the author. Too many adjectives can distract from, rather than enhance the portrayal of a character. Many new authors try desperately to convey what they are seeing in their own imagination. Descriptions are important but in small doses. The reader can do the rest. At the same time, it is important to portray your protagonist (and other characters) so the reader forms a clear image throughout the book.

To further develop imagery, do it through "show, don't tell." For example, a character can utter a phrase in dialogue that offers good visuals:

"Audrey, you look like you've been through a meat grinder. My God, your eyes are swollen."

Or, *"Bill, you know I hate handlebar mustaches. Shave that thing."*

Or, *"What's the matter, baby? You look like you've seen a ghost."*

Or, *"Geez, Sam, I can't get her out of my mind. Those eyes, like sapphires, her voice, like a sweet whisper, never angry, always caring. What a woman."*

Instead of writing: *Audrey had red hair and wore a slinky blue dress*, write: *Bill couldn't get his eyes off Audrey's red hair and her slinky blue dress.*

Often, a description can come from the character's actions, as in:
Audrey looked into the mirror and saw dark circles under her eyes and lines so deep around her lips she looked twenty years older than her forty-two years.

Sub-characters usually emerge within a story who support the main character or somehow propel the story line directly or indirectly. A main character has a spouse, friend, mother, adversary, neighbor, or other people in general who make up the mosaic of the novel, none of whom are as important to the story as the protagonist. Sometimes, authors will use (or overuse) a best friend or a psychologist character as a convenient person to whom the protagonist can open up, thereby informing the reader of his/her inner feelings. Virtually all novels have sub-characters. Be careful not to introduce too many or the protagonist gets lost in the crowd.

In *The Upside to Murder* I used a secondary character – a seasoned homicide detective who was nearly, but not quite, as important as the protagonist. As the story moves along in parallel chapters, the reader follows the paths of both men, the prey and the predator, at the same time. These characters also have significant persons in their lives who propel their individual struggles and motivations. Dr. Orville T. Madison has his wife and a daughter who had been the victim of a vicious assault. Detective Ray Blocker is a lonely man who fights internal politics in his department and manages to find love from a most unsuspected source. The two men come together in a climactic scene later in the book, but never is anyone more important to the story than Dr. Orville T. Madison. Without him, there would be no story.

Names for Characters

When reading a novel about Bob, John and Jim, and Mary, Karen and Linda, (yawn) it takes a while to root the image of each character into the reader's head. The names are so common, nothing stands out. Who wants to read a character scene with several people talking as follows:

> *"I'll pay the money tomorrow,"* John said.
> *"I want the money now,"* Jim responded.
> Bob answered, *"What money are we talking about, Jim? I mean, John?"*
> Jim looked at John who looked at Bob and John said, *"I'm confused."*

Think about some of the most interesting books you've read and check out the character names. For the most part, they are unique, unusual and memorable. Who can forget Scarlett O'Hara in *Gone with the Wind*? And Rhett Butler. Or Ebenezer Scrooge from *A Christmas Story,* whose very surname has become synonymous with grouchy old men. Sherlock Holmes, Sir Lancelot, Madam Bovary, Hannibal Lecter – those names instantly form images in our minds. If Hannibal Lecter had been named Jim Johnson instead, he would not be memorable.

My friends made up a name for their daughter thirty years ago: Bricole. It was perfect to use for a strong female character in one of my books.

Construct names from combining two names together like Sara and Josephine, i.e., Saraphyne. That will lock into the reader's mind, especially when she's described uniquely as being tall, portly and foul-mouthed.

In *The Upside to Murder*, I wanted a special name for my African American physician protagonist, thus: Orville T. Madison. From page one, that character is unforgettable. So is his nemesis, homicide detective Ray Blocker. While the first name is fairly common, the second name is strongly masculine. The name for his victimized teen daughter had to be feminine and sympathetic, thus: Cassandra, or Cassie for short.

Don't hesitate to give a character a nickname if it's appropriate. In *Dire Straits*, the protagonist is Cuban detective

Miguel Estevez, married to an American wife. It's doubtful she would call him Miguel on a daily basis, but "Mike" was a perfect fit.

Orville T. Madison's wife called him "T" throughout the story, while everyone else called him Orville. As a term of affection, Orville called her "Lovey" most of the time, except when they had harsh words; then both used first names.

Consideration must also be given to regional setting. I doubt many people from New York City are called "Bubba" or that too many from Birmingham, Alabama, are called "Vito." (Yes, I'm stereotyping.) Foreign countries have name options that are indigenous, all of which can be found through the most wonderful invention since sliced bread: Google. Whatever you do, avoid using "Mohammed" for a Jewish character, or Moshe for a Muslim. Leroy doesn't go with a Japanese character, and Katsuhiko is not a good fit for an Italian. Names should fit the personality, culture and geography.

There are a plethora of sites on line to research lists of names, their ethnic fit and original meanings.

Children's books are another genre which is set apart from other books when creating names. Their characters are often animals or unique people, and giving them names is a creative endeavor indeed. The most successful children's books are replete with inventive names: Harry Potter, Dr. Seuss, *Alice in Wonderland*, and so forth. Let your creativity go wild when naming characters in books for children.

Dialogue

People talk to each other. Sometimes they talk to themselves. They talk on the phone, they pray to God, they mull over their mother's voice, they argue, they even think aloud. Writing dialogue for a group of people can be tricky. The author must ensure that the reader always knows who is doing the talking, without necessarily identifying that person each time.

Dialogue is where the reader learns a great deal from what the characters say to each other, or to themselves. As much as reasonably possible, it is important to show, not narrate. Most novels have an omniscient narrator who provides most of the descriptive substance, but the actual feelings and action comes from the characters. Therefore, dialogue is essential in providing imagery to the reader.

The first and most important rule of writing dialogue is to separate paragraphs for each speaking character. Never include Bill's comments and Audrey's comments in the same paragraph. The separation of paragraphs defines the speaker to the reader, whether the paragraph is two words or ten sentences. Here's an example of the wrong way versus the right way, with identical dialogue.

"Oh Bill," said Audrey. *"You know I've always loved you."* Bill replied, *"Yes, I know, and I love you." "But Bill, what about your wife?"* Bill's expression changed. *"Don't worry, I've killed her. We're free." "Oh, good,"* Audrey sighed.

Here is the same dialogue, correctly separated by paragraph:

"Oh Bill," said Audrey. *"You know I've always loved you."*
Bill replied, *"Yes, I know, and I love you."*
"But Bill, what about your wife?"
Bill's expression changed. *"Don't worry, I've killed her. We're free."*
"Oh, good," Audrey sighed.

Another rule of dialogue is to use capital letters sparingly. A capitalized word denotes shouting or loud noises. The overuse of capitals is amateurish and can diminish the perception of shouts in the story. It is as effective to say: *"Bill, where are you going?"* as, *"BILL, WHERE ARE YOU GOING?"*

Regional or foreign accents are another element of dialogue often problematic with new authors who try too hard to make the reader hear the sound of the voice. You can inject a couple of misspelled words for accent effect, and the reader will get the message. Overuse of dialect and accents can be very distracting, and they appear amateurish.

Here is an example of dialogue with too much versus just

enough accent:

Miguel Rodriquez was irate. *"What eez zee mahta weeth you, senor?"*
Or, *"What is the matter weeth you, senor?"*

By denoting pronunciation with a single word, the reader can then processes the character's voice in general.

A southern accent may sound more like:

"How 'bout y'all don't a talk about mah mama?"
Or, *"How about y'all don't talk about my mama?"* The single word "y'all" covers the base. That's all you need.

What happens when a character is speaking then quotes someone else? Can you install quotation marks inside of quotation marks? Yes, but not the same marks. Quoting within quotations is accomplished with single quotation marks, as follows:

"You know what my wife said to me? She said, 'Tom, I am leaving you.' I couldn't believe it."

Profanity may be necessary in some books, particularly in police/suspense/mystery or military genre because you want to portray the characters as they truly talk. Criminals and gangsters, cops and sailors rarely speak in refined terms. At the same time you can overdo the expletives to the point where people simply won't keep reading. It's profanity overkill. Once, at a critique group, I reviewed a few pages of a new author's manuscript and criticized the writer, constructively, of course. In a single page the "F" word and the "MF" word were used at least twenty times each. Such terms completely distracted from the story, and comes across as unprofessional.

Most readers of mystery and police procedurals do not enjoy reading a constant barrage of foul language. While you must portray gross characters accurately, be wary about losing readers with gratuitous profanity.

Point of View (POV)

A point of view refers to the perspective from whom the scene is being felt, seen, heard, tasted or smelled.

When he opened the door, the lights went out. Immediately, he saw McGirk standing there with a scowl on his face. A guttural growl could be heard in the distance. Bill well knew the smell of fresh blood which had permeated the room. He was overcome with fear.

This opening sentence is related by the omniscient narrator from the POV of the character, Bill. In it, we are referring to four of Bill's heightened senses, i.e., sight, smell, sound, and feelings. No one else's senses, only Bill's. The reader then feels and sees what Bill is feeling and seeing.

Let's take the same scenario but change the POV to McGirk.

McGirk turned out the lights the moment he watched the door open. There was Bill, turning his head to the growling sounds from his Rottweiler. He knew Bill must have smelled the fresh blood around the room. Bill seemed very frightened.

That is McGirk's view. The same basic story is shown from two different sets of perception. It is important to remain consistent in using the same POV as you write a scene.

Think in terms of movie scenes. Every time a scene is portrayed or it changes time or setting, it is constructed from one actor's point of view. Likewise, a novel must always present scenes from the point of view of a character, even if the book moves from place to place and character to character. When you present a scene, use the point of view of the character from whom you want the reader to see and feel. Mixing POV in the same scene from one character to another will confuse the reader.

Mary Higgins Clark is a successful author whose trademark is short chapters. That's because she creates a new chapter every time the POV shifts to another character. Other writers, like me, may write two or three scenes (or more) within the same chapter. Those scenes are separated by triple spacing. When doing so, it's commonplace to install an icon centered on the space between the scenes.

In *The Upside to Murder,* several chapters are divided into two or three scenes which depict parallel happenings in different places, thereby creating varied points of view. Doctor Orville T. Madison, the protagonist, is the focus of attention by Detective Ray Blocker, and the book repeatedly switches back and forth between them. In most novels, you will see shifting points of view from one character to another. Notice that each scene remains true to a single character.

The exception may occur in novels that are written in first person. In this case, the narrator and the protagonist are often the same. Each scene is viewed from the position of the first person narrator, using pronouns; I, me, myself, mine. Ninety percent of novels are written in third person, giving the writer many points of view from a variety of characters to tell the story.

Using Tenses

Tenses are a device for showing time, thus informing readers whether a scene or event has occurred in the past or is occurring in the present.

The majority of novels are stories told in the past tense. Example: *It was a dark and stormy night.*

However, some writers prefer to write in the present tense:

It is a dark and stormy night.

Simply change the verb from *was* to *is*.

Writing present tense and/or past tense is the prerogative of the author. My preference is to tell a story as it happened, not as it is happening. To my liking, it is much easier to relate a story much the same as we relate stories verbally, in person over a dinner table, or to an audience. In writing novels, it's a matter of injecting the "now" or the "past."

Example: Audrey says, *"I don't feel good."* Then she opens the door and storms off.

Same event in past tense: Audrey said, *"I don't feel much like going out."* Then she opened the door and stormed off.

The biggest mistake new authors make is mixed tenses, using

present tense in one paragraph then past tense in another. It is essential that the entire story be told in a consistent manner (dialogue excepted). If you are using terms such as *had, did, went, was,* then continue to use them throughout. Don't change in midstream to *has, doing, going, is.* That's the sign of inexperienced writing that will not impress agents.

Setting

Every book has a setting or settings. Simply put, setting is the location of the scene or the broad environment in segments of the story. The setting in ninety-five percent of Stephen King's, *The Shawshank Redemption,* was a state prison. In *Doctor Zhivago,* we experienced many aspects of the Russian life during the 1917 Bolshevik revolution, from metropolitan Moscow to the rural landscape in the harsh winter.

Settings can be rural farms, raging rivers, city streets, houses, concentration camps, police stations, department stores, night clubs, outer space, foreign countries – wherever characters live, go or return to.

The reader becomes attached to a setting because it anchors a story to a specific place. In Hemingway's, *Old Man and the Sea,* the majority of the book is set in a small craft in the middle of the ocean. In *Gone With the Wind,* Margaret Mitchell created Tara, the southern plantation which became vivid with color, scenery, sights and smells, to the point that it is a common pseudonym for modern day country estates. The primary settings for Mario Puzo's, *The Godfather* were in the city of New York and the villages of Sicily. Yet, in *Godfather II,* the settings of early New York City brought us back to the turn-of-the-century and all its apple carts, horse-drawn wagons, early movie houses and Italian immigrants.

Settings are provided to the reader through the omniscient narrator and through the eyes and ears of the various characters. New authors should be careful not to over describe. Authors want the reader to see what the authors see in their imagination and often make the mistake of droning on. Here's an example of over describing:

While the rock band played noisily and the girl in a white dress and red high heel shoes sang a song from Lady Gaga, Bill wore a sharkskin suit while sitting on a hard chair at a round cocktail table lifting his stem glass which contained a martini made with Tanquery gin.

A shorter version:

Bill sat at a cocktail table sipping a martini, listening to the rock band and a female singer's rendition of a Lady Gaga song.

We don't need to know the shape of the table or the color of the singer's shoes. The term "rock band" implies loud music, because they all use amplifiers in their performances. We know that already. Providing descriptions in small doses allows the reader to fill in the blanks and get a good picture of the scene. Here's another example:

As soon as Bill reached the dark alley, he leaned over to tie his shoe, but avoided a puddle which was three feet in diameter, so he stepped around it. That's when two guys jumped him, a black man and a white man. The black man punched his stomach while the white man punched his face, then he fell down and the black man kicked him while the white man stole his wallet, and they cursed him before running away.

Or this:

As soon as Bill reached the alley, he was jumped by two men, one white, one black, who beat him to a pulp and took his wallet.

Same story, fewer words. Like trimming a steak, less fat, leaves room for more meat.

Plot

Think *struggle.*
Most novels are about the struggle of a character (or characters) in dealing with or solving a problem. A plot is what happens in the story, the order in which it happens and the

resolution.

Elementary as it may sound, most novels have three major segments: *beginning, middle* and *end*. That is the arc of a story.

The beginning should set the stage for the reader to want to read further. The main characters are introduced and the general story line is presented. It could be a crime scene, with the detectives and or victims serving as your primary characters. It could be an act of violence, a sensual encounter or a horrific accident that propels the remainder of the plot.

Example: A beautiful day of skiing in Aspen, Colorado is ruined when Bill slams into a tree, leaving him paralyzed. His new wife, Audrey, only twenty-four years old, is devastated. As the story follows, she is torn between loyalty to her crippled husband and her physical and psychological needs as a woman which may now never be met. The physician who treats Bill is unhappily married and falls in love with Audrey. They decide to cleverly euthanize Bill so they can live happily ever after. A sharp detective follows leads and unveils the plot, resulting in an international chase that ends up in a Colombian jail cell. That's where Audrey is killed by the doctor to shut her up, but he leaves an item of evidence, a hypodermic needle, which is traced to his DNA. An exciting chase ensues to the ends of the earth until the doctor is apprehended in a New Zealand cave. And so it goes. (Hmm. I just might start another book.)

The beginning grabs the reader. Each chapter, each scene, braces the reader for more, more and more. The characters come alive. The reader wants to know what happens to each sub-character, and of course, how it progresses into a satisfying or suspenseful ending.

The skiing accident is the hook. As soon as readers know Audrey is affected with doubts about her relationship, they develop mixed feelings about her, sympathy for her situation, but anger that she becomes disloyal to her disabled husband. She is the protagonist throughout and drives the course of the story, the arc, from beginning to end.

In my book, *Call Me Mommy*, the story begins in 1964 with a young woman (Laura) being wrongly sent to a mental institution by a wicked husband, leaving her baby in his custody for several years. When she finally is released, the small child has developed a five-year relationship with his stepmother and does not accept Laura as his mother. As the little boy grows, he is fraught with emotional problems and turns to drugs, becoming a lifelong addict. The story is told in incremental periods of the boy's life until he is a grown man, rejecting Laura as his mother, but giving her a grandchild to love and be loved by. The ending is highly emotional, bringing together the misery and struggles endured by Laura and her son at the hands of a selfish and depraved man whose actions early in the book severely impact the lives of every character.

Through the course of any novel, you will use dialogue, setting, motion and imagery throughout. Something should be happening at all times, whether it's a lone character reflecting on past events or mobs racing to catch a train. Keep it moving.

Epilogues

Epilogues follow the final chapter and allow you to sum up loose ends. In summary form, you relate what ultimately happened with the primary characters and sub-characters, that is, if you have not already done so in the story. I used epilogues in *Beyond the Call* and in *The Upside to Murder* to keep the story moving at a consistent pace, which did not leave time, or room, to describe the final outcome of everyone's life. There were many characters in the story the reader would care about. If you have written a compelling novel, the readers will want to know: What happened to Bill? What happened to the baby? What happened to Audrey's mother? Did she survive the cancer? Did she divorce Bill? Who got the money?

The epilogue can be wrapped up nicely in a few short sentences for each character. Do not go into long paragraphs of boring chatter when you can get to the point otherwise.

Your book may have thousands of words, but it is important that you accomplish the task with the fewest words possible.

Chapters

New authors ask: When and where do I draw the line in dividing chapters?

Answer: Whenever you want. There is no hard-fast rule. As mentioned earlier, Mary Higgins Clark wrote separate chapters from every scene. A scene might only consist of a single paragraph, thus, a very short chapter.

I have found most authors generally like to break the story into easy-to-read segments with one to three scenes in each chapter. The opening chapter of *The Upside to Murder* is a short scene about a boy finding a shoe on the beach with a human foot inside. It is a stand-alone scene, not immediately related to another even going on at that time.

Other chapters have as many as four scenes, because those scenes are running parallel to the story line of things happening at the time and/or place. Example: While Jane is having an affair with her lover in her bedroom, Bill (her husband) is driving home early from work to surprise her with flowers. Part of the paragraph is told from Jane's point of view. After triple spacing (for separation), the next part is told from Bill's point of view.

Chapter twenty-three of *The Upside to Murder* presents four scenes from various points of view, but they all interlock.

Readers involved in a story usually wait until they finish a chapter before they put a book down. So, don't even think about having no chapters at all. They are important divisions which help make the read more orderly.

Human Senses

The five standard senses are smell, taste, touch, sight, and sound. There are two more for authors: feelings and thought.

These are the senses that you, the author, are going to provide about each character in their individual POV. Use them wisely.

Think of any scene or encounter you have read in a book; they almost always include sensual descriptions. In dialogue, the characters see, hear or touch each other. You instill realism by using senses, which all readers can relate to.

Bill alerted to the distinct aroma of bacon frying in the kitchen. He could feel the saliva explode in his mouth. Then he heard Audrey holler in her distinct German accent, "Bill, ven are you coming to breakfast?" The minute he walked into the kitchen, he saw that she was nude, smiling, her eyes alive with desire. He was shocked, yet delighted.

"Forget breakfast, my darling," he said, grabbing her hand. "Let's go upstairs."

Bill's heart pounded with anxiety when the phone suddenly started ringing. Oh no, he thought. Not now.

"Answer the phone, Bill," she said.

"Phone? What phone?" he answered as he lifted Audrey over his shoulder and raced to the bedroom.

Feelings are not something you can touch, hear, smell, taste or see. But they are certainly an important part of a human story, so it's expected that you use appropriate adjectives for the moment, i.e., frightened, elated, embarrassed, anxious, guilty, cold-hearted, angry, submissive, and so on.

"Thought" is another aspect of using senses. When your character is thinking, this is outside of the five physical senses, but still an important part of the writing journey.

Example: *Mary plopped in her chair feeling deep despair and loss, thinking she would never again find love in her life.*

Or: Bill took another swig from the vodka bottle, thinking; *Does she really hate me? Is she going to kill me for my money?*

Without overdosing on sensual adjectives, be sure to relate the senses your character is experiencing.

Descriptions

The omniscient narrator has license to provide the reader with general descriptions of setting and characters, though it's good to leave some of that to the characters themselves. Providing descriptions is like an artist painting a picture. Use just enough paint of one color or another, and not too much of another. In other words, it is a special talent to know when to write enough and when it is not enough.

Do not overuse adjectives. Too much describing can sound gratuitous, and it interrupts the flow. Readers can be given tidbits of description and then they can fill in the blanks as their own imagination explodes.

The man looked homeless, unshaven, his eyes half closed and his crumpled pants appeared like they had not been washed in months. The closer he came to Bill, the more he smelled like a sewer.

That will do it. Readers get the picture without a full page of description. Readers do not need to know what brand or color of shoes the man was wearing, unless the shoes were significant to the story line. We don't care if he had tattoos or scars…unless, of course, they played some important role such as a witness describing an offender. The description was just enough. No more, no less.

Another mistake by new authors is the tendency to editorialize. Readers care what a character thinks about a situation or a person. Readers **do not** care what the omniscient narrator thinks. If the narrator writes: *The man was a total jerk,* you must ask, whose point of view is this? If it is the narrator's point of view, then he/she is editorializing, giving an opinion that comes from no character in the story. If the line is written, *Bill **thought** the man was a total jerk,* then we have a character POV.

Adverbs should be limited as well. Writers often use adverbs to modify verbs and clauses which give the reader a little more descriptive information. They are mostly associated with adding "ly" to the end of an adjective.

Careful - Carefully
Loud - Loudly
Soft - Softly

Besides overuse of adverbs, the most common mistakes by writers are the back-to-back adverbs, such as: *The man ran incredibly quickly.*

Or, *Fortunately, the unlikely promotion was happily accepted.*

A good author will reread his manuscript several times along the way and catch these problems. The overuse or repetitive use of adverbs do not have a good sound to the reader and are easily corrected. Surely, you smartly caught the joke laughingly.

Redundancies

While too many adverbs don't sound good, the same goes with redundancies. Simply stated, a redundancy is a matter of repeating yourself. Redundancy means using the same words and/or terms over and over when other choices would provide variety and make it sound much better.

During rereads, check your sentences and paragraphs for repeated use of the same word. On the previous page (under Descriptions), there is a sentence about a bum. Note how the word, "looked" was used in the beginning of the sentence to depict the man and the word "appeared" was used later in the same sentence to describe his crumpled pants. The word "looked" became "appeared" to avoid redundancy.

Editors pay particular attention to redundancies because they are a sign of amateur writing which, in turn, lessens the chance of getting published. Other examples of redundancies are:

It was a true fact.
A fact is purported to already be true.
Better to say: *It was a fact.*

It was a free gift.
The word "gift" already implies "free"

Here are a few more examples: *Final end; look back in retrospect; frozen ice; ancient old saying; tiny bit; plan ahead; big giant; unexpected surprise,* and so on.

"ATM Machine" is redundant, because the letter "M" stands for machine, therefore you're actually saying *"Automatic Teller Machine Machine."*

Same with PIN number, which is saying *"Personal Identification Number Number."*

A common overuse of a single word is "was." In many inexperienced writer's essays or books, you will often find a disproportionate number of sentences beginning with: *"He was; She was; It was."* For an experienced reader, they stand out like an "aching, sore thumb." (Oh wait, that was redundant.)

Try to avoid constantly telling the reader that Bill was meticulous or Mary beautiful. Once you've conveyed that to the reader, it doesn't need repeating. However, if there is something exceptional about the scene, you can always write more specifically, *"Mary didn't have a hair out of place. Bill's heart raced at the very sight of her."*

Book length

Keep track of your word count. If your book is over 100,000 words, it is too long. Most first-book novels are somewhere between 60,000 and 80,000 words.

Traditional publishing companies are not going to risk investing in an expensive book with a no-name author. James Michener and Stephen King can get away with it, you can't. There is no novel that cannot be pared back to a shorter story if needed; it only takes creative editing. If some of your best writing has to be discarded, that's life.

Look for those scenes, characters, actions, etc., that are not important at furthering the story line and delete. It may hurt, but you'll get over it. And the book will more likely be considered by an agent.

Bear in mind that a thick book over five or six hundred pages is going to be much more expensive and less likely to sell in the marketplace. It will be hard for publishers to sell and for you, the author, to sell.

An ideal book length for a new novelist is around 70,000 to 80,000 words, give or take a few.

CHILDREN'S FICTION

Writing for kids is an entirely different field. Much depends on the age bracket you are targeting. Children's books for kids three to eight years-old are usually about super heroes or animals. That's when an author uses wild imagination in telling the story with out-of-this-world characters. Such was the successful Dr. Seuss series that has fascinated tots for forty years.

Writing for older kids nearing adolescence requires a little more realism in characterization; otherwise kids will feel like they're being treated like…well, kids. The most successful children's writer of all time is J.K. Rowling and her myriad of science fiction fantasy characters in stories centered around a young fellow named Harry Potter.

Writers should be focusing on children's books that will sell modestly in a saturated marketplace. Besides good writing, all children's books need pictures and illustrations. This is where the costs rise.

In ninety percent of children's books, authors need to include illustrations along with text on many, or all, of the pages. Unless the authors are artists as well, they will need to contract with an artist or co-author the book, as many have done.

Consideration must be given toward the quantity of illustrations and the use of black and white versus color. More pictures equal more pages. The more color, the more dollars.

Getting a small children's book published with twenty or thirty color illustrations raises the cost significantly. For self-publishing, it doesn't matter if you are willing to pay the invoice. For traditional publishing companies to offer a deal, they will consider their production costs first.

Children's books sell well, particularly at certain times of the year. But there are downsides. It's all up to you.

5

WRITING MEMOIRS

LIFE EXPERIENCES

Memoirs and detailed autobiographies are cathartic for people who feel they have a lot to share with others, whether family and friends, or readers in general.

Be prepared to relive some poignant experiences because they will become vivid once again as you pound the keyboard. War veterans will relive the horrors of battle, death, dismemberment, misery and terror. A police officer will think about those times when innocent little children were abused, battered and killed, or when he held a dying partner in his arms. The gunshots fired on you or your partners will play back in your mind. You will see the blood and hear the screams once again in your head. The fireman's nightmares from scenes of tragedy will resurface. Doctors, nurses, emergency responders and crime victims must be ready to deal with the memories they have buried for a long time. Love and romance will come back to life as vividly as in 1957, as will the joys of children and other profound sources of happiness. Tragedies you experienced in life will touch the heart as though they happened yesterday. Be prepared to relive all these emotions because that's what memoirs evoke: fears, joys, heartbreaks, anger, disappointments, suffering and struggles.

Revisiting the past is not a bad thing. By writing about those events, authors often come to terms with their emotions like never before. Writing is like a form of therapy, an awakening, a positive, unintended consequence of the book-writing endeavor.

Memoirs can be written about a single event or set of events, or they can cover a lifetime of highs and lows, careers, travels, love and family. It all depends on your particular goal.

My friend and author, James T. Joyce, wrote his memoir, *Pucker Factor 10,* about flying helicopters in Viet Nam. In one of his most vivid memories of everyday life during that war, he wrote of dealing with the rats. Yes, rats! They were everywhere, at every camp. They came back to life as Joyce detailed the struggles of a soldier from Chicago in Southeast Asia. It's a great book for readers who want to understand one man's struggle through an unpopular war.

Joyce wrote his book and then two more memoirs mainly because his adult kids wanted him to. They will be enjoyed and treasured by generations to come.

In 2002, a small, elderly man named Robert Body self-published a book titled, *I Survived The Bataan Death March.* It told of the brutal treatment of him and thousands of prisoners by the Japanese in World War II. While attending a book fair, I listened to Mr. Body at the podium trying to speak about his story, but all he could do was cry – sixty years later. By professional standards, the book was poorly written. But it didn't matter.

WHY MEMOIRS?

Memoirs are generally written for one of two reasons:

1) For posterity – to entertain and inform family and friends
2) For commercial enterprise

If you were a president, a movie star or a wartime general, or if you had sex with the president, you'll sell a lot of books because you're famous with a following of millions.

If you are not a famous name, forget about commercial success unless you measure success as a few hundred books. Most people will not pay fifteen or twenty dollars to read a book about someone they never heard of, unless there is a special hook: You met alien creatures that landed from another planet; you accurately predicted the future for a hundred people; or you died and witnessed heaven and then came back to life. Writing about the aroma of Grandma's apple pie or watching your kids graduate high school are not unique examples of life happenings that will produce sales.

People generally write memoirs to share with their kids and grandchildren, for their friends and friends of their friends and for future generations. These memoirs are usually written by seniors who have assembled an interesting history of experiences and being retired or semi-retired, have enough time on their hands to dedicate to such a project. People of all ages care deeply about ancestors and yearn to know more about their lives, struggles, personal talents and idiosyncrasies.

My memoir, *From Violins to Violence*, primarily written for posterity, turned out a surprising success by my standards, meaning it sold about 3,500 copies. By Stephen King's standard of selling millions, it was a colossal flop, but to me, a success. I was amazed that a few thousand people who never knew me would care about my story. Then again, word of mouth is like a virus if the stories are compelling enough and the writing is good.

While I am not a famous celebrity, the book caught on because readers were fascinated to learn how a wimpy kid who played violin and grew up in a family of Miami Beach mobsters ended up as a career cop working in Miami-Dade Homicide. I like to think some of the sales success was due to an active and effective marketing campaign. One good thing about autobiographies, they are never out of date. We still read about people's lives from centuries past.

If your goal is to make money off your memoirs, be sure you have a "hook" that will draw readers away from other authors. In other words, write what others have not written. Experiences like spending five years in a Siberian prison, or finding out you have parents from Mars, or you are a man who became pregnant, are worthy of book sales. Books about growing up in middle class America, playing sports, being the best cheerleader or being able to fix cars or play saxophone – if that's it – will not be in high demand by Barnes & Noble booksellers.

It is important to know *why* you're writing your life's story.

Your expectations should not be unrealistic. You should know that profound dedication and concentration will be self-imposed and a myriad of emotions will be unleashed. Ideally, you will have a spouse or partner willing to share your commitment with patience and understanding. Remember, it doesn't matter if you don't sell a lot of books. What's important is getting your stories into print – while you still can.

I encourage all people who have arrived at their golden years, and who have the time, to write their memoirs. Men and women over seventy years of age have lived a long life with many experiences stored in their brains, all destined to oblivion when they pass on, lost to the ages unless they are recorded. It doesn't matter how well your memoir is written. What matters is that it was written at all. With memoirs, the reader is forgiving.

LEGAL IMPLICATIONS

I have often been asked about the risks of liability if an author wants to name people in an unflattering manner. Can the author be sued? Good question, indeed. The answer is: Yes. Of course, anyone can sue anyone for anything, but few lawyers will waste their time unless they think they have a chance at winning. In order to win, the plaintiff must claim and prove damages, that he or she was injured in one way or another. Here is what I know without consulting an attorney for more specific details.

Rule One

The dead cannot sue. In most cases, you can write almost anything (that is accurate) about a dead person. If you want to expose dirty details about a deceased acquaintance from years back, go for it. Be sure you are correct because families of loved ones can make life miserable for you if they discover inaccuracies and they think their spouse, father or son has been defamed to the point that it caused a negative impact on their businesses and personal reputations. At the least, your credibility will be damaged and no one wants that kind of embarrassment. The bottom line: Never write anything about anyone that is not true. That's as basic as it gets.

Rule Two

If the subject of your criticism is alive and able to claim you have defamed him/her, be very careful in your writings. When writing my memoir, I learned it's all right to use pseudonyms for characters you don't want identified by name. Assign an asterisk to the fictional name and indicate in the beginning of the book – perhaps the preface – that any asterisks found by readers are meant to be pseudonyms. In my memoir, I identified Max Berman as a corrupt cop in the 1960s. I did not reveal his true name because he was still alive.

If you criticize a living person, be prepared to support your allegations with irrefutable records and/or witnesses which pose as a mighty barrier to avert legal repercussions. If facts are common knowledge, you're on steady ground. You can call anyone a murderer who has been convicted of the crime. However, if someone has been charged and not convicted, then it's wise to use the term, "alleged" murderer to avoid law suits. If it is well known that a local cop was caught and admitted using illegal drugs, he's fair game for being exposed for that act.

Professional authors like Edward Klein who write exposé books have available interviews and sources from which they acquired information. In his new book *The Amateur*, Klein excoriates President Barack Obama with a litany of criticism about his conduct in office, all of which he claims is verifiable from named and unnamed sources. If sued, he could reveal his tapes and his sources, which the president would probably not want. Knowing that, the Obama camp ignored it.

PHOTOGRAPHS

Authors of memoirs tend to overkill with pictures. Because there are so many stacks of scrapbooks from years past, it's difficult to discern which should go in and which to leave out. Celebrities load up the photo section of their books because they have so many famous friends to show off, young and old, outside of their own family tree.

It is good for autobiographies or special experience memoirs to include an assortment of historical photographs (with captions) of family members, old cars and buildings, a picture chronicle of one's life, so to speak.

Most pictures are placed in the center of the book, usually about ten or twelve pages depicting the author as a child, later as a young adult, family members, the marriage, the career and then the extended family. Add in a couple of notable personalities the author may have met or known like politicians or entertainers. Photographs are always an enhancement; readers like to put a face to characters and the places you write about.

The quality and number of pictures you add to a book depends on how you are having it published. Cost is an important consideration. A traditional, mainstream publisher will look at the cost of production before committing to a certain number of photographs. The publisher will also have to decide whether it's worth publishing photographs in color (very expensive) and on glossy paper (also expensive) versus text paper (the least expensive). Memoirs produced by standard publishers do not often have many pictures, unless the author is a famous name and certain to sell books in the multi-thousands. My memoir has twelve historical photographs on six sides, on text paper only. That was fine with me.

You can self-publish a book with as many pictures as you wish, providing you are willing to pay the extra printing expense. Remember, self-publishing companies are in business to make money much the same as traditional publishers. They pass the cost of production on to the author. The problem with higher costs is the inability to makes sales at an outrageous retail price per book. If you want a memoir to sell, do not price it over $20.00.

Here are a few rules to follow for including photos in a memoir:

1) Don't include pictures of people unless they are mentioned in the text. Readers look at the pictures to put a face on the characters you write about. Adding pictures of old or obscure friends who are insignificant to your story will not be of interest to the reader and a wasted cost. But...it's your book.

2) Use captions. Identify who's who, where and when, below each photograph. Readers like a sense of time and setting.

3) Limit your photo count to about a dozen, give or take four or five. If you have a rare set of captivating pictures about famous events like battle scenes, African famine, presidential elections, additional photographs will be acceptable.

WRITING IN PHASES

There's a lot of flexibility in spacing a memoir. It's totally at the discretion of the author.

If you are writing a full life's story, it's good to divide the book into chronological phases, usually four or five, maybe more, such as: Growing Up in Brooklyn, Off to College or Military or Living In The Streets, Making a Family, Enjoying Retirement, and so forth.

These are only generic suggestions. Everyone's life is different. Within those phases, you can subdivide into chapters according to the periods and events you are covering. Readers subconsciously look for order in the writing, which is why we have chapters, phases and subheadings.

One ploy some authors use to "hook" the reader is to start a memoir with an exciting or poignant scene from the center of one's life, then return to the beginning of the story in Chapter Two and work chronologically from there. A war veteran may start out by describing the scene of one of the battles he fought in Viet Nam, when he saved his friend's life in the jungle in the face of the enemy, the fear, the sweat, the nerves, the sounds and shrills. These events are unforgettable for an entire lifetime and give the beginning of the book a snapshot of what the author is all about in mid-life.

In *From Violins to Violence*, Chapter One begins with a mid-career scene in 1966, titled, "A Cop's Toughest Job." In it, I tell of being a young detective suddenly bestowed with the responsibility of informing a young mother that her son had drowned. I'll never forget her instant transition from smiles to utter grief. From there, the book reverts back to the start of my life.

It doesn't matter how long your chapters are as long as they are centered within the basic title of that particular period in life, i.e., *Hanging Out in High School.* You don't want your stories of

Viet Nam battles mixed in the same chapter as taking your girl friend to the school prom.

Be liberal in using paragraphs to keep the reader organized in thought and process. Long, uninterrupted text is like a wall of words that creates a blur, tiresome to the reader no matter the content. Just check out the formatting of this book and you'll get the idea.

PACKAGING A MEMOIR

In Chapter Three, we covered the various methods to publish a book. Unless written by celebrities, most memoirs will not be of interest to major publishers because they would not create enough sales to cover the cost of publishing and marketing, yet make a profit.

That leaves three methods:

1) Print On Demand publishers
2) Self-Publishing houses
3) Do-it-yourself

Print-on-demand publishers may not charge you any money, but they usually expect you to agree to buy a minimum number of books at the wholesale cost. Naturally, the wholesale cost is inflated so the publisher can make a healthy profit. This normally entails the purchase of at least one-hundred books or more, depending on how many you think you'll sell on your own.

Self-publishing companies usually produce a quality product, but they pass the cost on to you, the author. Set-up costs for self-published books can run authors anywhere from $500 to $5,000, depending on size, quality, cover design and the requisites of the specific company. Then you purchase books at their designated wholesale price, usually about forty percent discounted from retail.

Both POD and self-publishing companies provide cover designs, assign ISBNs and get your books listed in online book store systems. It is a book like any other book, only the selling process is mostly up to you.

Do-it-yourself is just what it means. Print your pages and put the material into a folder, binder, or notebook – any way it stays together.

Several years ago, I spoke at a church about writing memoirs, encouraging everyone in the room to give it a go. A few people took the advice and assembled old photographs, letters, documents and writings about the good old days. A year later, an elderly friend named Sid was proud to lend me his new book. It was a store-bought, three-ring, four-inch notebook, thick with pictures, old documents and manuscript text about his life. That was good enough for him, and good enough for his friends and family. It was certainly good enough for me. If he had wanted it to be a little more sophisticated, he could have had it spiral bound at a local retail office store for a small price.

The main thing: his memoir is now preserved for all time.

DOs AND DON'Ts OF WRITING MEMOIRS

Before you sit down to share your life with the world, you must be psychologically prepared. Know that this process is going to bring a great deal of your past emotional time clock to the surface. Some writers are not prepared for such a very personal experience. Writers will share much about their emotional struggles, including pain and suffering, traumatic events, loves and losses, bitterness and affection, accomplishments and regrets. The degree to which you reveal your personal life is strictly up to you, but there are guidelines that everyone should follow, or at the least, be aware of.

Here is a list of DOs and DON'Ts for writing your memoirs:

DO:

1) Include stories and events about family, friends and associates who mean a lot to you, and to whom you mean a lot. People like to read your thoughts and feelings about others, as well as yourself.

2) Try to write as many positive and complimentary comments as possible about the people who deserve them.

Name your mentors and how they guided your life the most. Express love.

3) Share your pride and what you feel were your major accomplishments, not so much the end result, but the journey getting there.

4) Tell of the most heart wrenching personal experiences, if possible. The more you share inner feelings, the closer your reader will feel to you.

5) Use emotion as a trigger to get people wanting to read more, your fears, your loves, your struggles.

6) Share what you learned from your experiences and what deserves to be passed on to others.

7) Use the senses to describe settings; how did it smell in the cabin kitchen, the spectacular colors of autumn in the mountains, the feel of cool rain, the sound of a baby laughing, the taste of food in other countries, deafness following an explosion, etc.

8) Confess your regrets, if you are ready and willing and what you would do differently.

9) Keep the flow moving as it is a story, like any other story, only your story.

10) Share what you missed most in life, what advice you would have for your grandkids, and your so-called "bucket list," what you would like to have accomplished.

DON'T:

1) Use a lot of inane dialogue. Except in situations that warrant a direct quote, readers are not going to follow "he said" and "she said" back and forth. Save that for novels.

2) Bore the reader with petty disputes you had with others, unless they created a life-changing situation.

3) Resort to derogatory name-calling. If you had a husband who cheated or abused you, tell of the abuse, but omit, "that son-of-a-bitch" or "he was a low-down rat." Let readers reach their own conclusions based on the facts you share in the book.

4) Whine and sound like sour grapes. If someone else got promoted or was treated better than you, tell how it affected your life or the lives of others, but try and suppress the anger. Readers are not there to take sides; they just want to know you better. Find something positive from the experience, or forgiving, and how it eventually improved your life.

5) Write boring technical or personal health details. You may be a gun or a computer expert, but the average reader doesn't need to know the intricate construction of a MAC 10 rifle or a MAC hard drive with all the components. Nor does the reader need to know how many strokes you use brushing your teeth or why flossing is good for you. If you want to write chapters about your general health, diet supplements and exercise, then write a non-fiction health book, not a memoir.

6) Over gush. The tone of your writing will convey your feelings about wife, husband, mother or children to the reader. Constantly referring to how much you loved (or disliked) someone can turn in to overkill. Those feelings are important, but try to do more of *show, don't tell.*

7) Overlook segments of your life that would be most interesting or compelling, like visits to faraway places that are off the tourist maps, or interacting with people of another culture, or how it felt to save someone's life, physically or spiritually, or how someone saved you. It's good to be humble, but not to the point where you omit

significant highlights.

8) Use real names of living people who could claim they were offended or damaged, and bring you to court. If you write negative opinions about others or claim they acted improperly, immorally or illegally, do what you can to conceal their true identity. Do not reveal secrets that were entrusted to you unless you have permission in writing from that source.

   (Note: in *From Violins to Violence*, I truthfully referred to my stepfather as a bookie and a mobster. If he were alive, he would probably be unhappy with that. Because it was such an interesting aspect, it was included. Bernie is dead, the era is long passed.)

9) Fail to complete the story. If you've written about a primary character in your memoir, let us know the outcome. Caring for a sick spouse for many years is an ordeal, and the reader wants to know if she or he lived or died. Use an Epilogue at the end of the book if that works best for you.

10) Be inaccurate. If you write about people, events or situations in a manner that is grossly slanted or untrue, the words may come back to haunt you. Credibility for a writer is everything. Remember, once your memoir is in the marketplace, anyone may read it.

11) Reveal too much about your own life's indiscretions. Sometimes, you can be *too* honest. There may be incidents or portions of your life no one needs to know. People will not miss what you don't tell them.

STRUCTURING YOUR MEMOIR

For the sake of this subject, we will assume you'll be writing a memoir that will be published in a traditional format, whether self-published or major league traditional. For people who intend to assemble a homemade notebook as a memoir, some of the following will not necessarily apply:

Format

For organizational acuity, you should consider the following:

1) Write in chapters.
2) Give a name/title to each chapter, i.e., "Mom's Ordeal" or "The Accident."
3) Keep the story chronological...unless you use flashbacks (which can be tricky).
4) Include a Table of Contents which lists the chapter titles and page numbers.
5) Include a Preface. Many authors write this after they've completed the book. Though it is placed at the beginning, reveal what or who inspired you to write the book. It is always good to bestow appreciation and special love to a spouse, mentor or other loved one.
6) Dedicate the book. I dedicated *From Violins to Violence* to my great-granddaughter. You may wish to dedicate the book to a mentor or parent who influenced you the most.
7) Select ten to twenty photographs for the center of the book, or other places if you choose, always noting who is depicted, and when/where if appropriate.
8) Keep the book to a reasonable word count, 60,000 to 90,000 words, but no more than100,000 words. Extremely lengthy books are costly and pose a deterrent to readers.

Good Advice

Before going to press, think about sharing your manuscript with one or two persons close to you, either relatives or good friends, especially those who are named in the book. Personal feedback from an inside perspective can be valuable. Most memoirs will include serious and stressful periods of your life and will almost always entail mentioning others. If a dear family member might be offended, embarrassed or disappointed with what you have written, or the memoir contains information that should remain private, you might want to consider rewriting those segments.

When you write about yourself, you are also writing about others who might care very much about what you are disclosing. Telling about an alcoholic mother or an abusive father – deceased or not – may be a catharsis for the author, but it could place a sibling or an offspring into an awkward or uncomfortable position. Consider their feelings. That's when the author decides what to edit out before it goes to press. When the book is available in the marketplace, it is too late. Give thought to and use discretion in what you reveal.

6

THE NON-FICTION BOOK

Writing is writing. Whether you write fiction or non-fiction, you still must convey messages, write tight and provide information in a readable format with as few errors as possible. Poor writing and errors in syntax and punctuation distract the reader. It's like running smooth and fast, then suddenly stepping into quicksand. It takes a few minutes to return to a pleasant gait again.

The biggest difference between fiction and non-fiction is you're not making anything up in non-fiction. You're either telling a true story and/or you are providing knowledge and information of interest to readers.

Non-fiction covers an endless array of subject matter and methodology, much too extensive for this small guidebook, but we'll cover the main points. Many other outstanding books in the marketplace offer tips to aspiring non-fiction authors. Here are a few:

On Writing Well: The Classic Guide To Writing Non-Fiction by William Zinsser

Writing Successful Self-Help and How-To Books by Jean Stine

How to Write Your Own Life Story by Lois Daniel

Writing Non-Fiction: Turning Thoughts into Books by Dan Poynter

CHOOSING THE TOPIC

Know your target readers, and write what you know.

My friend and author, Stu Borton, owns an upscale restaurant in Palm Bay, Florida. Borton is a class chef who assembled an array of recipes and photographs in his publication, *The Yellow Dog Café Cookbook*. He is renowned in local Florida circles for providing quality food to fine diners who frequently return to his restaurant, particularly for special occasions. His target readers are men and women who want to cook fine and unusual recipes. He knows his readers and he writes what he knows.

Non-fiction writers generally don't *choose* a topic. The topic chooses them by default, much as it did with Stu Borton. Authors who write non-fiction know a lot about something, which most other people know little about (hopefully) so there is a market for sales.

Doctors, lawyers, accountants, psychologists, hobbyists, historians, military officers and other professionals write what they know best in topics that fall within their purview of expertise. Their credentials help to sell a book. I could not write a book about aerodynamics, meteorology or plants and mushrooms, even if I knew more than the average person. I have no credentials or experience in those fields. I do know a lot of baseball trivia, but who cares? No one, outside my immediate circle of friends and family, would buy a book on baseball by someone with no credentials in the subject.

There are two basic categories of non-fiction: Narrative and Informational.

Narrative (story telling) is much the same as fiction in terms of text, format, grammar and syntax. The author tells about a set of actual events, an exposé, or a biography about a person or organization that is famous or worthy of note. If you are writing about a true story, tell it without embellishments or half-truths, and without a biased slant, if possible.

Significant omission is a tactic for slanting a factual story to manipulate the reader's mind in alignment with the author's. Authors who did not like Presidents G.W. Bush, Jimmy Carter or others, write heavily about the negatives and often omit the positives. The same in reverse when authors favor a John F. Kennedy or a Barack Obama.

If I want to make you believe that Ted Bundy was a really good person who suffered from child abuse, I would write heavily about his charming accomplishments and education and write less about his killing more than thirty women. Authors have the power to affirm readers who have a predisposition for feeling a certain way in advance of reading the book. Or, they have the power to sway readers to a new point of view, depending on how effective they are at identifying their sources for information.

Christian authors write about biblical people and events as though they were confirmed fact, while contrary readers may challenge most of the information. If the reader already wants to believe the content, it's a done deal no matter what.

Those who write glowingly about the history of Islam often omit the violent or hateful verses in the Koran and emphasize the peaceful text. Nor do they tell the entire biography of the Prophet Mohammed. Writing with omissions can be very effective in swaying believers to any point of view.

Informational writing can be text books, science studies, diet, health, history, how-to, travel, motivational or essays from politics to religion to art. This guidebook, *So You Want to Write a Book,* would be classified under the non-fiction "How-To" category.

Besides memoir authors, story tellers generally have a specific set of events they wish to convey, like Robert Body who wrote about the Bataan Death March. Many people have sold tons of books by writing about their personal dealings with celebrities like Marilyn Monroe and President Clinton. They primarily exploit the celebrity aspect. Selling is what matters. Monica Lewinsky didn't sell her books because she had a sexual encounter with just anyone. It was about *who* she had it with. She is not considered a first-class author or a special person in the public eye, but her dalliance with the president provided her an opportunity to become a one-time, hot selling writer.

My friend and fellow writer, Holly Fox Vellekoop, lost an adult son to cancer after two-plus years of suffering. Later, she penned a heartfelt and informative non-fiction book, *How To Help When Parents Grieve*. The title speaks for itself. To relate such a tragic story, the author had to live it.

Mark Fuhrman, the former Los Angeles detective, wrote about the double murder which O.J. Simpson was charged with: *Murder in Brentwood*. Who better to tell the story than someone who was in the investigative arena?

Vincent Bugliosi was the prosecuting attorney in the murder cases that sent Charles Manson to prison for the bloodthirsty spree that killed four people in Southern California in 1969. Who better to tell the tale in *Helter Skelter* than the person who knew the case inside and out?

In non-fiction accounts of any event, the most important factor is accuracy. Be prepared, if needed, to attest to your account of the story, that it was witnessed by yourself and/or others, that you have interviewed people or researched publications where people are quoted and investigator's reports are recorded.

I learned this the hard way. After my book, *Militant Islam in America* was published, a columnist reviewed it in the local newspaper. She praised the writing and admired the plethora of information, but issued scathing criticism for the book failing to cite all sources. The book did name many sources in the text quotations along with a bibliography in the beginning, but I did not provide footnotes and index attributions. When writing about a controversial subject, I learned how important it was to attach all sources of information.

Informational or "How-To" non-fiction, first and foremost, requires author's credentials. In other words, what makes you an authority? Credentials can be inserted in your author bio and elaborated upon within the Preface or Introduction, as you wish. Readers want credibility, to know they are reading from someone who knows the subject matter inside and out. Where did you learn how to do sculptures? What schools did you attend? What galleries have featured you? In what restaurants have you been a top chef? How many years were you in homicide? How long have you been practicing civil or probate law? Accounting? Neurosurgery? Fixing jet engines? Archeological digs in Egypt?

Most non-fiction authors specialize in some endeavor or career path that sets them apart from the average "Joe." Military war veterans, career astronomers, retired or current politicians are all able to produce impressive credentials. Some of us are dabblers, but not experts. Though a writer may have excellent taste in unique foods, or knows a lot about fashion design or landscape work, none of that necessarily makes him/her an authority on the subject. But I am trained in classical violin, I worked sixteen years of a thirty-year police career in Miami-Dade Homicide and I have studied crime and justice system from the inside and the outside my entire life. I feel fully qualified to write non-fiction on those topics.

Here are a few rules in writing non-fiction:

1) Maintain credibility.
   All it takes is one inaccuracy and your book is spoiled like a roach spoils a good cup of chowder. The remainder won't matter. Check your facts, ensure they are true and supported with personal knowledge, the knowledge of others and/or records.

2) Quote accurately and in context.
   Short quotes should be exact. Long quotes don't have to be verbatim provided they convey the intended meaning.

3) Cite sources.
   Either in text or in an index, provide resources that can corroborate allegations and/or purported facts. In text, it's permissible to say; "According to Barack Obama, in his book, *Dreams From My Father*..." Or, with very detailed non-fiction, it's wise to use footnotes. When citing an opinion, simply state, "It is the opinion of this author that..."

4) K.I.S.S.
   Keep it simple, stupid. Unless you're writing a thesis for a Ph.D., or a text on scientific matters like forensic chemistry, pretend that you're writing as a high school junior and scrap the big words that you think make you sound intelligent. Get to the point and move on without belaboring...like I haven't done in this paragraph.

5) Avoid clichés and metaphors.
Save that for creative writing. Facts do not need clichés and metaphors. Ex: Fit as a fiddle; In the nick of time; All that glitters is not gold; and most appropriately, read between the lines. If you must use a metaphor, be original, create a new one.

6) Use clear terms and fewer words.
Instead of saying, *"He made financial gains of considerable quantity,"* reduce the language to simpler terms, *"He made a lot of money."* When you look over your manuscript, consider how you can tighten the prose by eliminating words such as *then, but, just, really, very, and, anyway.*

7) Tell the story, not *your* interpretation.
Readers will spot bias right away. If the story is credible, you do not need to add inflections. Let facts and ample description of happenings speak for themselves.

8) Spell correctly.
Elementary, my dear. Spell-check does not correct wrong spelling for the intended meaning. Ex. *"She came form behind."* (I hope you caught that) Or, *"He bought stamps at the past office."* Spell-check will not catch correctly spelled words in incorrect context. (Haven't we said that before?)

9) Write tight.
Keep sentences short. Long sentences drag on. Same with paragraphs. Use the "Enter" key liberally to keep the reader reading.

10) Proofread.
A poorly written book, no matter the content, is often a turnoff to avid readers. Be sure you check every page, every sentence and every word for syntax, construction, punctuation and flow. Have an experienced and objective reader check over your manuscript. Better yet, pay an editor to do it right.

Finally, too many new authors blunder by repeating the same thing, again and again. It's redundant to be redundant; therefore, you should be redundant in checking your redundancies. Should I repeat that?

This is true for any form of writing, whether fiction or non-fiction.

GETTING PUBLISHED IN NON-FICTION

If you intend on pitching your non-fiction book to a standard publisher (other than memoirs), they will have specific guidelines to follow which are different from fiction. The specifics of each may vary from one to another, but there are a few common requirements:

1) Don't finish the book – yet.
   You should *not* write a non-fiction manuscript before you have first written a book proposal. No publisher will read your manuscript until the proposal first passes through an agent.

2) Prepare a chapter by chapter outline of your entire book, with short summaries of each chapter.

3) Write a proposal, much like a synopsis, which is to sell your project to an agent and ultimately, a publisher. This can be anywhere from three to ten pages, double-spaced. It should contain your credentials, background in published writing, target readership of your book, how and where you expect an interested market, what the book contains that makes it different from other books in the same genre.

4) Submit queries, with proposal and chapter outline, to agents who handle your genre. Follow their guidelines for submissions, which will vary from one agent to another.

If you are self-publishing your non-fiction book, you can disregard the guidelines under this subheading. You will not need an agent nor will you be required to sell the concept to the publisher. However, some self-publishing companies have standards that prohibit extreme violence, profanity and porn.

7

WRITING TIPS

GENERAL

Here are a number of basic writing tips to be considered, regardless of genre. While some of the following may be pertinent to one form or another, such as dialogue which is not generally found in informational non-fiction, it's good to keep these pointers in mind.

1) See the Movie: Formulate your scenes as though you visualize a motion picture. Keep the movement flowing, capture your reader with curiosity about the next page, the next chapter, the scenes, the excitement, the struggle, the conflict.

2) Minimize the Ridiculous: Be careful of extreme implausibilities. We all accept that fiction allows the author literary license to create super human deeds, but be wary of the ultra extreme. Ex: It's an acceptable coincidence that a police detective would bump into the very criminal he's hunting at a local Walmart, but it would be off-the-chart if he bumped into him while vacationing in Sydney, Australia. Neither is it likely that a human will survive a fall from the Empire State Building, no matter the shape he is in. You're not going to find a fingerprint on the trigger of

a gun that's been buried in mud for five years. When you make readers moan in disbelief, you've lost them.

3) Investigate: Do your homework. If you want to know what a true-life Crime Scene (CSI) investigator does on the job, contact your local police and arrange a ride-along. Interview police and crime scene people, or physicians, or garbage men, or anyone else with expertise in your situation. Being guided by what you view in television and movies is a big mistake. Crime scene investigators seldom, if ever, make arrests, engage in shoot-outs, question witnesses, and the females certainly do not wear stilettos and low-cut blouses. This same principle applies to other plots, settings and characters. Dig deeper than what CBS and NBC provides you. In *The Upside to Murder*, I queried a licensed pilot to learn details of a small, single-engine aircraft. He also taught me some of the technical aspects of flying.

4) Science Fiction: This is the exception to Number 2. Depending on the nature of your wildest scenes and characters, anything is possible. Readers expect the impossible. Science fiction and fantasy open the door to the most preposterous extremes of imagination.

5) Sex/Violence: Keep graphic sex, violence and profanity to reasonable levels. The average reader may enjoy a hot and juicy scene here and there, but gratuitous sex and continuous foul language cheapens the writing, and the reading will get old fast. If your story requires sex and vulgarity, use it in moderation.

6) Inconsistencies: Make sure your story is consistent. If a character is twenty-nine years old in Chapter One, and only a few days have passed in the story, be sure it coincides correctly when she gives her birth date in Chapter Seventeen. A blue Maserati cannot morph into a Lamborghini in different sections of the book. And, if the victim was killed with a .380 caliber handgun, be sure the

bullets are the same caliber when they are recovered in the autopsy. Long manuscripts approaching 100,000 words can play tricks on the author's memory bank when it comes to minor details.

7) Killing Kids: Unless the core issue of a fiction story absolutely requires it, avoid writing stories in which children and animals are killed. It's troublesome. Some readers will put a book down immediately when a sweet, eight-year-old child is killed, or a villain shoots a Cocker Spaniel. If the killing of a child is central to the plot and the follow-up suspense, that's understandable. But if the killing is gratuitous and you can insert a different victim in place, do it.

8) Flashback: If you are going to write in flashback, be sure you have read Sidney Sheldon or other authors who use that tactic. Flashback is effective in many books, but doing it correctly can be a challenge. Study, learn. Don't speculate. Do it right.

9) Time Frames: If your book involves many periods of a lifetime, be sure to keep the reader informed. Using subheadings in chapters is effective and saves explanation in the text. For example:

March, 2012, Three Years Later
Back On The Farm, March 2012
The Next Morning – 6:25 a.m.

Build the time frame into the text, i.e., *"The fall colors were in magic brightness now as five long months had passed since Abigail lost her husband."*

10) Authenticity: If you write about a convict's life in prison, visit a prison and see what it is like first hand, the sounds, the smells, the depression. If you cannot actually travel to a foreign country depicted in your book, venture out to meet a native from that country. Ride with cops. Interview

doctors or nurses. Get permission to view an autopsy. Sail in a yacht or cruise boat. Skydive. Fight whitewater rapids. Know what you are talking about.

I once critiqued a new writer's manuscript in which her female protagonist is violently raped in a public bathroom inside a toilet stall. As described, it was totally implausible in a physical sense. That doesn't mean the author should have first been victimized in such an event, but it did make me wonder if she was very inexperienced.

11) Writer's block: It happens to most of us. Being immersed in a writing project is strenuous and consumes enormous concentration. At times, the brain shuts down and fatigue sets in. That's the time to put down the project for a couple of days, for a week, a month…maybe a year. Even if you are on a deadline, your mind needs a rest from the pressure you have imposed on yourself. The book is saved; it isn't going anywhere. Take a few days off. Exercise. Drink. Read another book. Make love. Travel. Do anything but write.

12) Memory: You may get new ideas in the middle of shopping at the mall, telling yourself, "Don't Forget that!" Or, while you're teeing your ball on the golf course. Or, while out to dinner on a date. Later, you're back at the computer and you totally forgot all those ideas. In the old days, we kept a pen and notepad handy. In 2012 it's even easier. Carry a small voice recorder with you at all times and verbalize your thoughts on the spot. Forgot your voice recorder? Call your house and leave a message to yourself on voicemail. (Yes, there's a solution for everything.)

13) Organizing: If you're a Type A personality and everything must always be organized, create a detailed, chapter by chapter outline of your book and set a schedule for writing at the same time every day. If you're a Type B, wing it and get going when it feels right. You may write ten hours one day and one hour the next, all at different times of the day,

but it doesn't matter as long as the job gets done. Keep the outline of your story in your head. Visualize the movie.

14) Quirks: Drink coffee. Drink wine. Listen to music. Keep the room dead quiet. Dim lights. Bright lights. Whatever works for you. Write down ideas while you're pounding the keyboard. Create a miscellaneous document on the Word program and note ideas as they come to you. Write naked. Wear a golf hat. Stay warm. Have a photo of a loved one in sight. Keep tissues handy. Take breaks often. Walk around the block to think, bring your voice recorder. I told my grandson that the most important tool for my writing, besides the computer, was a backscratcher. Yes! Feels good.

15) Save. Save. Save.

CRITIQUING YOUR MANUSCRIPT

As you work on your first book, have someone you trust look over your manuscript at the halfway point, or earlier. You'll want someone who can do an objective reading and provide you honest feedback and criticism. While your mom or your spouse may have made good grades in English, that doesn't necessarily qualify them as a reviewer of a full book manuscript. Far more goes into a critique than looking at punctuation and spelling.

As you read and re-read your manuscript, look for words that can be eliminated without losing essence, such as too many adjectives and conjunctions – *and, but, then, however, so, anyway, just.* If the sentence says the same thing without that word, it is superfluous and eligible for the "delete" key.

Be wary of thin skin. You should welcome criticism. If your feelings get hurt too easily, you're delving into the wrong business. Never argue, explain or defend. You have the last say in what stays and what doesn't in the manuscript. It's your book.

WRITERS ORGANIZATIONS

While writing can be a vocation and commercial venture for

authors, it is also a personal pastime for millions of people throughout America. Some call it a hobby. Others call it a passion. An ambition. A calling. Call it what you want. To express themselves by the written word is an important part of people's lives.

Just about every city and town in America, except those with a population under ten, have established writers organizations of various size and composition. You can find most by using "Google." These organizations are comprised of support groups and educational forums; they may hold monthly meetings with speakers, special seminars and important critique groups. Some host elaborate conferences at local hotels which feature expert speakers and attract agents and publishers for sit-down reviews with local authors. Many authors have signed with agents via the contacts made at conferences.

The best advantage to writers groups is the networking and friendships established with other authors. Much can be learned from each other. Signing up with one of these organizations generally costs a nominal annual payment for dues, which also gives you access to their monthly publications and/or newsletters.

New authors: Join your local writer's organization. You have everything to gain, and nothing to lose but around $30 or $40 a year.

CRITIQUE GROUPS

A good critique group can be very helpful. A poor or inexperienced group may do you more harm than good.

While I have experienced all of the above and met many new friends after I started my writing career, nothing came close to the value of being part of a high quality critique group. My mistake was not joining such a group until I had already published my first book with a POD company and was working on my second.

I was very fortunate to be accepted by a critique group consisting of one major-league published author and two retired English professors, one of whom headed the English Literature department at a major university.

Our group of five authors had its own system:

1) Meet every two weeks at a neutral location, such as a library room.
2) No alcohol or social amenities; this is not a social occasion.
3) Each writer distributed a few pages or a short chapter of a work-in-progress to other members. Those pages were reviewed and critiqued at home by each writer over a two-week period. The critique included a short written report highlighting what was perceived as problematic, whether in style, syntax, punctuation, plot, characterization, setting, etc. At the next meeting, writers took turns critiquing each of the submitters. Each writer did not necessarily have a submission prepared at every meeting. There were usually two or three critiques per meeting.

Attending these sessions was like receiving a college education in the dos and don'ts of writing books. Participants not only helped me edit, I absorbed their knowledge and expertise in formulating plot and making characters come alive. I have since joined other critique groups, but none of that same high caliber.

Other critique groups work differently. Some writers do not want to take the time to prepare written critiques, no matter how brief. They simply determine what's important and relate the issues verbally at the next meeting.

At some meetings, critique groups read aloud from a full or partial chapter and then expect others to critique aloud, one by one, immediately after. This may be better than nothing, but certainly not ideal. Some people cannot fully concentrate on a verbal reading, thus much is overlooked or omitted in the critique.

How your group structures the critiques is a matter of consensus. I heartily recommend all new authors participate in such a venture, no matter the format.

For critique group participants, here are two important bits of advice:
1) Be honest yet diplomatic with the author you are critiquing. You may not say what another writer wishes to hear, but your credibility as a critic is rooted in candor. At the same time, be liberal with compliments wherever they are

deserved.

2) Don't get your feelings hurt. Don't argue and don't be defensive. Always thank your critics, consider their input and then do what you darn well please.

Critique groups are usually spawned from writers organizations in your local community. They are very beneficial if you are joined with professional level writers who know what they're doing. The experience can be damaging if members of your group are not proficient readers or skilled writers. They may give you bad advice and/or fail to point out important problems which you may ignore and fail to correct. Most writers organizations are generally composed of good authors who have been around a while and know right from wrong in the composition of a manuscript.

Critique groups work best when the members are working within a similar genre, so that novelists are not critiquing "how-to" books. Finding the right people in your basic genre is not always easy, but it is important.

PUNCTUATION

Writers can obtain books on the finite details of writing a manuscript, including punctuation. If you are interested in highly detailed information about line-editing, find another book. This segment will touch only on the most common problems and rules of line-editing that a beginning author should know. Bear in mind, most of my knowledge did not come from a classroom or a book, but by trial and error, my personal editors and those wonderful critique groups.

Periods

Yes, that's a little dot (.) at the end of a sentence. (puhlease)

Commas

Use commas when a pause is needed for clarity, providing there is a need. Without that comma between "clarity" and "providing," the sentence would present an entirely different sound.

Use commas following introductory words, phrases and clauses. Ex: "But, that would be okay."

Exclamation Marks

Read this, now!

Such punctuation is used to, well…punctuate! Exclamation points are meant to stamp *emphasis* onto a comment or denote a raised voice, often in dialogue. Use them sparingly.

"I hate you!" "Watch out!" "I've had it!" They are often used at the end of a shouting comment: *"Get out of here or I'll kill you!"*

A non-question beginning with "How" or "Why" might require an exclamation mark, such as: *"Why am I such an idiot!"*

Question Marks

If you have any questions about when or how to use this item (?), first learn the difference between a statement and a question. Every question, whether dialogue or in narrative, ends with a question mark. Is that understood?

Huh?

Apostrophes

1) Apostrophes shorten the verb, such as "is" and "not." Ex: *"For he's (he is) a jolly good fellow."* Or, *"Why haven't (have not) they arrived?"*

2) Use apostrophes as a short contraction for a word: Aren't = Are not. Can't = Cannot. For the most part, books with good writing have fewer contractions and more words spelled out. Dialogue is an exception, as it depends on how the character speaks.

3) Use apostrophes to indicate a possessive. Ex: *"The lady's purse."* Some writers mistake plural for possessive as in: "The ladies purse" which is incorrect. "Ladies" denotes more than one lady.

4) Apostrophes are often used at the end of a word ending in "s" to denote a plural or singular possession. Ex: *"Charles'*

bike was stolen." Note, we did not Charleses.

Semicolons and Colons

A semicolon has been called "a comma with a degree." Often, a semicolon may replace a comma in long and formal sentences.

Semicolons are used to separate two main clauses, as in: People who write novels hope for readers; people who write memos hope for raises.

Sometimes, a writer will use the term "however" in the middle of a sentence, which should be separated by appropriate punctuation, as in: *'Peter felt good; however, the feeling did not last long."*

A colon (:) is used to set off a summary or a series. Ex: *"Peter was faced with four problems: an angry wife, missing kids, no money and a fatal disease."*

Dashes

A dash – like this – can be used effectively in place of parentheses to interrupt a thought with a relevant piece of information. Ex: *"Peter had a number of illnesses – besides financial problems – which led to his suicide."*

A dash can be used at the end of a sentence to accentuate the final word or phrase: *"Peter fixated on the final outcome – death."*

Parentheses can be substituted with dashes at the whim of an author. Ex: *There are numerous Muslim countries – Saudi Arabia, Yemen, Somalia – that practice strict forms of Islam.* Parentheses could also have been used. You decide.

Parentheses

Parentheses can be used in a number of situations, like clarifying a number. Ex:*"The total cost exceeded seven hundred dollars ($700)."*

Use parentheses when noting information as an aside, within a sentence. Ex: *"Peter returned to Miami (quite unexpectedly) to see his ex-wife."*

A parenthesis can be used to enclose a number or letter used for establishing a list. Ex: *There are three ways to read this book: (1) in text, (2) on Kindle or (3) as audio.* Letters can be used in the same manner: (a) (b) and (c).

Sometimes an author might enclose a segment of a paragraph intended to better explain a confusing situation. *Peter returned to Ireland in order to meet his relatives. (Actually, Peter was never in Ireland except as a small baby.)*

Hyphens

Hyphens are used in common connectors and numbers, such as: right-of-way, forty-five years old, a stand-up guy.

Hyphenate spelled out fractions, i.e., one-third, four-fifths.

Hyphenate all compound words beginning with "self," i.e., self-employed, self-respect.

Prefixes and root words that join two vowels may (but not always) be hyphenated, i.e., re-entered, co-owner, semi-invalid. Other double-vowel words do not require hyphens, i.e., coordinate, reemployment. (Don't ask me why, I only work here)

Ellipses

Ellipses are three dots (...) that signify an omitted item, an extended pause, paraphrasing a quote or a trail-off ending of a sentence. Here are some examples:

1) "I pledge allegiance to the flag...and to the republic for which it stands."
2) "Peter stepped cautiously through the door and looked down...hesitating."
3) "What the...?"

With ellipses, you may eliminate other punctuation, such as commas.

Quotation marks

We mentioned the use of quotations in the dialogue section of Chapter Four. It is important to go over the rules because new authors often fail to use quotation marks correctly. Here are the basic rules:

1) Any quote, whether from a character speaking, part of a speech, or from another previously written document, always begins and ends with double quotation marks, i.e., *"Four score and seven years ago..."*

2) If your long-winded character speaks for more than one paragraph without interruption, do not use a quotation at the end of that paragraph, but start the next paragraph with double quotation marks again. At the end of the entire recitation, close the quotes.

Here is a shortened version:

"Three times in my life, I have been on the edge of death, ready to meet the maker, suffering, weeping, but I still prevailed.
"If it was not for Doctor Jones, I wouldn't be here today."

3) For quotes inside of quotes, use a single quotation mark. Ex: *"Peter said to me, 'Mom, I love you.' That meant a lot to me."*

4) Periods and commas go inside the quotation marks. Ex: *"I saw Peter with a gun," John said. "But it wasn't loaded."*

Upper case vs. lower case

In first grade we learned that all sentences begin with a capital letter. We also learned that proper names, and names of places and titles of books should be capitalized, Ex: The United States, Paul Bunyan, Campbell's Soup, Rocky Mountains, *Gone With the Wind*.

Prepositions, conjunctions and articles are not capitalized in titles, unless they are the first word. Notice "the" in the movie title, previous sentence.

Capitals are not required when referring to a title not preceding a name, i.e. *"I saw the president."* When referring to The President of the United States, however, capitals are used. Same applies to all formal titles; *"the senator"* versus *"Senator Sam Jones."*

In the age of cyber writing, you may see capital letters for entire words in e-mails to denote shouting. DO YOU UNDERSTAND? In books, that's a no-no. All capitals should only be used in extreme situations which denote panic, or as in the famous line by Jack Nicholson in *A Few Good Men,* "YOU CAN'T HANDLE THE TRUTH."

Italics

Some new authors tend to overuse italics. A manuscript I recently reviewed featured an inanimate household object as a living character, observing all the happenings in and around from its perspective. The author wrote all the narrative from this object in italics. That was fine, until he started using italics in other narratives and quotations, which caused confusion.

Here are some basic rules for italics:

1) When referring to the title of a published document, book, movie, newspaper, use italics. *Gone With the Wind. The Upside to Murder.* The *Miami Herald. Phantom of the Opera.*

2) Unless "The" is a part of a title, it does not require italics. We can write the *Miami Herald*, without italics for "the."

3) Do not italicize long passages within a bible or other sacred works.

4) If a foreign word or phrase is widely used in the English language — such as the French, "bon voyage" or the Latin abbreviation, et cetera – we would not italicize it. This is a matter of personal judgment. Whether you italicize the Italian sotto voce depends on your audience and subject matter.

5) For dialogue in a foreign language, use italics. From *Dire Straits,* in a violent scene of robbery and murder by Hispanic drug smugglers, Javier ordered them in Spanish to search the house: *"Busca por todos lados. Me estoy ponieno impaciente."*

6) Use italics for special emphasis on a single word or phrase. "This is *not* what I expected." Or, "The main issue here is using *italics*, not underlines. Is *that* understood?"

7) Italics can be used to isolate a third party dialogue outside the context of the prevailing characters, as in a background voice from a television set. Ex: Peter hushed Sally and pointed to the television set where a newscaster was reporting.

> *"The police have not yet identified the shooter, but ABC News will keep you up-to-date with the latest reports."*

Long narrative of third party background voices should be indented as well.

8) Use italics to identify a non-verbal sound, such as a dog's growl: *Grrr.* Or a banging sound: *kerplunk.* Gunhots: *Bang, bang.*

9) Use italics for self-reflective thinking. *Why is she looking at me that way?*

10) Dreaming: *Wind soaring, rain falling, I'm running along a pier...oh no, Oh No! Wha...? Ahhhh.*

Note: Many times, an underline can be used as an alternative for italics in emphasizing a word, but they <u>should not </u>be overused.

Spelling and Misspelling

Naturally, it is important to spell correctly. But sometimes you might want to spell a word incorrectly, as I did previously: *Puhlease*. This is done to accentuate an accent or a deliberate mispronunciation. In one of my books, *Beyond the Call,* a redneck police sergeant has a drawl as he uses the term, *"Hey, Boah."* (Meaning, *"Hey, Boy"*)

To repeat, for emphasis; ***do not*** rely totally on your program's spell-check system. Many words may be spelled correctly but they are the wrong word for your sentence. For example, spell-check will not know which of the following words are meant for your text, because they are all spelled correctly:

Made – Maid – Mad
Here – Hear – Heart
Fellow – Mellow – Yellow
Steel – Steal
Form – From

"Wee ken ewes spell check!"

Numbers

As a general rule, spell out short easy numbers and use numerals for the longer numbers. A one-sentence example: *"Ten-year-old Billy did not understand his seventy-one year-old grandfather when he said he had just won $125,750.00 in the lottery."* We certainly do not want to read "one-hundred and twenty five thousand, seven hundred fifty dollars" in text. For street addresses and phone numbers, using numerals is best, i.e., "456 Elm Street." Otherwise, as a general rule, spell all numbers under twenty (20).

Manuscript layout

Most word processing programs have margins established by default, generally one inch on the sides and at one and a half inches from the top and bottom of a page.

Times Roman is the most common font, though I have been asked by one top agent to change my manuscript font to Courier New.

All manuscripts submitted for review by agents/editors/ publishers should be double-spaced. That is the standard requirement. This is especially important for critiquers and editors to allow space for hand-written notations.

See the sample two pages of manuscript at the end of this guidebook.

Bottom Line

Webster's Dictionary. Don't leave home without it.

8

MARKETING YOUR BOOK

Don't be too concerned about book selling if you have a major New York publisher who has provided you with a healthy advance and got your book reviewed in the *New York Times*. If you hit the major leagues, you just need to show up when and where you're needed (be prepared to travel). The publishing company will do much of the guidance and marketing with your help and cooperation, of course. Publishers expect you to do your share in the marketing process, whether appearing at book signings, radio shows, book fairs, or speaking engagements, and creating your own website.

For this chapter and for the majority of authors reading this book, let's concentrate mostly on writers who are published by smaller traditional companies, POD and self-publishers. That's where most of the selling is up to the authors, their energy and creativity.

ESTABLISH A WEBSITE

It's the twenty-first century. Authors must use websites for several functions:
1) Taking book orders on line (to sell)
2) Providing a brief biography of the author
3) Listing books, book covers, reviews and what they are about

4) Providing shipping information, ISBN, prices
5) Providing contact information to prospective book talk/signing events
6) Supplying a photo of yourself (and the book cover) for advertising needs

All these items will eventually be requested by book stores, libraries, news media and other venues where you will talk about your books. Your web site is a media package on-the-ready, for anyone interested.

Websites cost money, but it is essential for any author in engaging a marketing plan for sales. Many experts in the marketplace are ready to help you establish and maintain, a website – for a fee. If your community is large enough and you have a writers' organization, they will likely have someone who can help. Plan on spending at least $300, or more, to get it up and running. If you have several pages on the site, it will cost more.

Consider it a necessity.

MARKETING MATERIALS

As a new author preparing to market books, you will need:

1) A website (whoops, I already said that).
2) A boiler plate flyer for scheduled book talks and signings. This means you can use the same basic flyer from one event to another, just change date, time and location.
3) Bookmarks with your brief bio, photo of a book cover and a few blurbs about the book. These are usually 2 x 8 ½ inches but can be wider if you want.
4) A ready press kit available at the website or by standard mail. Press kits are information packets about you and your books.
5) Business cards designed to your liking. You *will* be using them.
6) A folder for all your news clippings and book reviews from which to make copies.

ORDERING BOOKS

Some writers of memoirs may only want to pass out copies to friends and relatives and keep a few on hand for gifts. These authors are not interested in sales, just the satisfaction of seeing the end product of their labors.

Selling is a different story. Don't count on publishers to do the marketing for you. They will usually have your book listed in catalogues, on their own website and on Amazon.com. That's it. No matter if you are self-published or with a traditional publisher, when your book is released you will need your own inventory via the publisher's established discount. Be sure to order enough books to sustain you for book talks and signings, plus some to send out to writing contests, newspapers and reviewers.

If you have written a novel or a self-help book and want to sell as many as you can, you will be busy attending a variety of functions. That will require your own inventory. Don't be stingy. Make sure you have a couple hundred books on hand. You can order more when and if you need them. Plan on giving some away to your family members and closest of friends. Expect to sign and send books to people who helped you the most, including those who provided your blurbs, plus people who you consulted for expert advice, without whom you could not have completed the book. It's the right thing to do.

PRE-PUBLISH ENDORSEMENTS

Before your book is actually published, try to secure one or two people with impressive credentials who can review your final manuscript and submit a glowing comment on your book. Those comments, even when paraphrased, can appear as blurbs on the front or back of your book.

The reviewer should have a background tied, somehow, to your genre. If you've written a police thriller, a blurb from a farm worker won't do you much good. Your mother or your English teacher won't do, unless your English teacher is an established author as well. Then, attribute your blurb as follows:

"– Maria Abernathy, author of *The Bird Never Flies.*"

For my novel, *The Upside to Murder,* I was fortunate to get a reading from an established attorney who was a former homicide detective and from an active Medical Examiner, in addition to another published author. Those people added impressive credentials to the reviews and the cover blurbs.

In the absence of "experts" in your genre, having another published author provide a reading/review is always an option.

If you are a member of a writing organization which includes authors, you can ask for volunteer readings and blurbs. Most authors are happy to see their names appear on another book as a reviewer because it validates their status. If you know someone with credentials in your specific genre, such as a military-based novel, and the reviewer is a retired Brigadier General from the U.S. Army, he will add credibility to the blurb. For most of my crime novels, I have obtained reviews from experts in criminal defense law, prosecutors, police chiefs and established authors. Be sure to let your publisher know you want those blurbs on the book cover or back page before it goes to print.

POST-PUBLISH REVIEWS

Talk matters. Readers usually buy books based on what someone else has said, primarily in published reviews and personal referrals. Everyone knows *you* think your book is great, but do other more objective people think it's great? There's the rub.

You will want to champion your book through the words of others. So, before you start making posters and inputting data to your website, make every effort to get published reviews.

For those published in the minor leagues, the high-powered reviewers in national newspapers will rarely open the front cover of your book. Who and how you are published matters a lot to the likes of the *New York Times*. They will not bother with minor league authors. You may get your book reviewed by your town newspaper because you are a local personality, or by a local periodical in your area. And if you have another home town where you grew up, the newspapers and/or periodicals there may be gracious in reviewing your work.

Don't be stingy. Your first book order should provide enough spare copies in inventory to submit to reviewers and writing contests.

Online sources are available for book reviews, though some will require a fee. Those reviews can be very objective, candid and useful in your marketing endeavors.

When other published authors assist with reviews and blurbs, be ready to return the favor later on if you are asked.

You could also ask new readers who compliment your book to write a few lines in the comments section of your listing on Amazon.com. People do read those reviews.

BOOK FAIRS

Check online or with your local writers organization for book fairs where a gathering of authors are assembled in one venue for a day or two to meet and greet readers and to sell and sign books. Major book fairs, like the International Miami Book Fair, are held annually, but they generally limit their participants to authors published in the major league market.

There are hundreds of other smaller book fairs held once or twice a year in communities throughout every state, sponsored by writers organizations and within writers conferences, for the same purpose: meeting, greeting, selling and signing. The author pays a small fee to secure a table (or half-table), usually around twenty or thirty dollars. It's a good idea to have items such as posters, flyers, business cards and bookmarks to hand out to customers whether they buy books or not. These are good venues to get your name familiar to the world of readers.

Book fairs differ in how sales are conducted. It all depends on who is managing the event.

1) Direct sales – author to customer
2) Retail intervention

Direct sales is exactly what it means. If a customer likes your book, you – the author – will sign the book and handle the money transaction. You may accept credit cards if you have the equipment on hand. You may accept checks if you choose, or accept cash and make change if needed. Sales taxes can be added, or built into the sales price and then reported as required by law for that state.

I have *never* used a credit card machine. In twelve years of book fairs and other book events, I can count on one hand the number of sales I lost because of the credit card issue. This is a personal choice.

I have been paid by personal check many hundreds of times and never had a bounce yet. The day I do, I won't worry about it because the reader probably needed the money more than me. Checks are still going to be around until my generation is long gone. People who browse book fairs and attend author talks are not your common check fraud suspects.

For most small-press and self-published writers, authors haul their own supply of books to the fair. Their profits are over and above their purchase costs from the publisher, plus whatever expenses are encumbered for gas and marketing materials. If a self- published book sells for $15.00, but costs the author $7.50 per book, that author will earn half the retail sale as profit (minus expenses).

Multi-published authors are smart to offer discounts as a lure for people to buy books. It's the same tactic used in retail: buy two books at full price, get a third for half price. In my case, I discount my older books that normally cost $15.00, to $10.00 each, with a prominent sign on the table. Books that sell for $17.95 can be discounted to $15.00. It's also easier for making change.

Retail intervention is another system for selling at book fairs, but it is far less profitable for authors. Book fair managers may use this method to expedite the flow of sales and provide a sense of order to the event. Having a name like Barnes & Noble to arrange event sales adds a bit of clout.

This always involves a retail enterprise and a representative from a book store. In this arrangement, the buyer meets the author, then takes a selected book to purchase at a central location where the store agent handles the sale. The buyer returns to the author's table for signing of the book. No money is exchanged between author and buyer. The author receives royalties from the publisher, which is usually dispensed to authors two or four times a year.

A ten percent royalty for a $15.00 book yields $1.50 for the author. Meanwhile the retailer makes about forty percent of retail, in this case: $6.00. If you have brought your own books to the fair, paying $7.50 each for your inventory, you will barely break even for the day, no matter how many books you sell. Some authors consider such an arrangement a way to get known. Others consider it an unnecessary rip-off. But it gets the author's name out to the world in dribs and drabs.

Selling through the retailer also eliminates your option to offer discounts because the bar code rings up the fixed retail price at the sales counter.

BOOK SIGNINGS

A book signing entails an author sitting at a table at a selected venue for a pre-scheduled appearance. It's up to you, the author, to arrange these events. Most of the time, these are at retail book stores. When the day is over, you will earn whatever royalties are due from sales.

Retailers like Barnes & Noble are not usually interested in hosting book signings unless the author is well known and/or the book has been well publicized. They want books to sell, not see an author sit for two hours behind a stack of unsold books. Usually, the retailer obtains books by ordering through a distributor and then provides them at the signing. Unsold books will usually be sent back to the publisher, unless you are a very popular author and the books will be sure to sell.

If the computer indicates the publisher's policy is "No Return," book stores will not likely agree to the signing because any unsold books cannot be returned to the publisher. Thus, the retailer gets stuck with the unsold books. This is a firm policy especially with self-published books and POD publishers. Some stores may work out a deal with the author, whereby the author brings copies of the book and agrees to pay a percentage of sales to the retailer and takes home the remaining unsold books. For the most part, self-published and POD authors are not invited to retail stores for book signings.

Book signings do not have to take place in book stores. I know a fellow who sold lots of his recipe books at beauty salons, waiting for ladies to come in the door, signing one book after another. He gave the salon a couple of dollars for every book he sold. Restaurants, civic centers, churches, craft shows, even country clubs, may host a book signing, depending on the deal you can make. It's all up to your perseverance, energy and imagination.

Whatever you plan, notify the local newspaper guru on books and authors, so he/she can insert a notice of your scheduled appearance. If you're lucky, you might even get an interview.

BOOK TALKS

These venues for book signings and sales have one catch: The author must give a talk. Such talks are generally scheduled for one hour with book sales and signings to follow.

When people are entertained by engaging in dialogue they are more likely to develop interest in your book. The most common location for book talks is a library. I have probably sold more books at library talks than all the other venues combined.

Libraries usually have an adult program director who coordinates events for artists and writers. Some have stringent rules about hosting authors who give talks. Some require a percentage of sales be given to the Friends of the Library, a non-profit volunteer group. Some pay a stipend to authors who they think will bring an audience. Some libraries do not allow sales on premises, while others do. It is important to clear up these issues ahead of time.

These talks are close and intimate with authors using a lectern if they choose. My style is somewhat loose, walking around and becoming friendly with the audience. Authors are expected to talk about their book, but also their writing regimen, their personal history, or the reasons the book was written. Writers who have a difficult time with public speaking might want to work on those skills before starting out. It's good to mix a little humor and interesting facts, along with questions and answers, and to find out if other writers are in the audience. In my case, I always look for criminal justice-connected people to cite when talking about laws, crime, violence, courts and corrections.

Don't be disappointed with small turnouts. Sometimes you can take a seat with an audience of three and have a friendly discussion in general about books and authors.

Some authors like to do readings, choosing a chapter, or portion thereof, from their book to read aloud. That works for some, but not for all. A reading can bore an audience if it goes on for more than three minutes. For me it's not an option. I never read aloud, except for an occasional rave review to help me brag.

If you are engaging enough and the host receives good reports, you will likely be asked for a return engagement.

Book talks do not have to take place at libraries. Men's clubs, women's clubs, book clubs, condo associations and civic organizations are all possible venues for arranging a talk about your book and its subject matter. If your topic is venue specific, like a non-fiction book on health care, or medical issues, you might contact local hospitals and universities. If you've written about insurance and investments, you can contact people associated with Met Life, State Farm and Edward P. Jones. My writing student, Bahia Abrams, wrote a superb novel about a love affair between a Jewish woman from Syria and a Syrian Muslim who's connected to a terror organization. *The Other Half Of My Soul* was especially well received in Jewish organizations and synagogues.

Again, when you schedule a book talk, notify the local newspaper, giving date, time, location and a brief (very brief or they will not read it) sentence about you and your book. If the newspaper wants more, they'll call you.

FAN LIST

If you plan on writing more than one book and speaking at lots of venues, you should start a fan base and keep a listing of your readers, names, addresses and e-mails. You can offer a link on your web site where fans can sign up to be on your mailing list.

Readers at talks and signings who bought your books and paid by check have already provided you their home address which is usually printed on the check itself. Start making a list and keep it up-to-date somewhere on your computer program.

I hadn't been to The Villages, Florida for a book talk in four years. When my new novel was released, I arranged a return visit. I went through my old mailing list from previous talks at The Villages and sent a number of people a note in the mail about my scheduled talk. Some actually showed up. Those notes cost me about four dollars in post card stamps, but I sold about $150 worth of books because of them.

WRITERS CONFERENCES

In the chapter titled, "Getting Published," we learned about writers conferences and the advantages to new authors for marketing their work. New authors should attend as many writers' conferences as possible. Most large and medium-sized communities host them once a year, usually through the local writers clubs. They are also listed on the Internet.

BLOOD SUCKERS

I thought it important to include this topic because new authors are susceptible to rip-off artists who are out to take advantage of the ambitions of the innocent and inexperienced. A host of marketing gurus out there will try to convince you of the wonders they can do if you are willing to part with a couple of thousand dollars, like listing your book in every catalogue imaginable for readers and movie producers to see. They'll say your chances of sales will skyrocket with all the exposure. The guarantees are huge, but if they don't pan out, well…"I'm sorry."

Some self-publishing companies hire employees to be your "marketing consultant." In truth, they may be low-cost foreigners sitting in front of a computer in an office cubicle somewhere in Mumbai, India, or the Philippines, trained to convince you that spending money to list your book at a book fair in Los Angeles will bring miraculous sales. All it will cost you is $350. Your book may be listed in Los Angeles all right, buried among thousands of other titles in catalogues which few people actually see.

Searching for good editors and publicists can cost you more than you can afford. Publicists in the major leagues command up to $10,000 a year for guiding an author to the right venues for appearances and book signings. High cost editors may charge authors up to $8,000 to pore over an average manuscript. However, there are plenty of experienced authors and/or former English teachers who enjoy reading and making a little extra money, charging much less while still providing a quality editing job. Again, finding them will entail networking in conferences and writers' organizations.

Hiring a publicist is a great idea if you're published by St.

Martins Press and expect to sell a million copies of your book a year. Then someone else will do your scheduling while you embark on writing another book without constant interruption and distraction.

Stephen King never has to make phone calls to set up book signings and talks, or design book marks and brochures. His managers do all that. Maybe, someday, you'll strike it rich like Stephen King, if you keep working and improving as a writer. Meanwhile, you'll have to do most marketing on your own.

CHILDREN'S BOOKS

Marketing children's books entails much of the same process as other books, with the exception that your target readership is anywhere between two and seventeen years of age. That bloc can be designated further into three categories: Pre-kindergarten (two to six), elementary ages (six to twelve) and teens (thirteen to seventeen). The one common thread between all such books is that they should be devoid of any references to sexual activity. References to violence should be curtailed to the teen set only, and – in my opinion – in moderate terms. Extreme and/or gratuitous violence in any children's book will pose as an obstacle for getting published in a traditional market. Even self-publishing companies frown on using sex and violence in children's books.

So, in addition to all of the above here are a few extra tips for selling your children's books:

1) Visit bookstores in person. Most retail bookstores will not order your books for their shelves, but they do engage in children's readings. Independent bookstores are particularly amenable to scheduling readings which can expose you as an author and encourage parents to order your books from the store. Independent stores may also agree to sell your books on premises, providing they get their forty percent. Parents like having books for their children that are signed by the author.

2) Libraries are a good venue for reading your book to children. Contact local libraries to schedule a reading or

presentation. The rules for selling books on premises vary with each jurisdiction. Library administrators are often in search of good programs for kids.

3) Schools are a good place to read and sell books, but much depends on the age group you target. Call schools and speak to librarians, or call parents groups, for arranging author visits. School representatives may offer to sell copies to interested teachers and children in advance of an author's appearance.

4) Senior citizen centers are an excellent venue for marketing children's books. Grandpas and grandmas are always looking for unique gifts to give kids, and books autographed by the author are very appealing. This is especially good in the month prior to Christmas or other special occasions.

5) Book fairs, as discussed earlier, are a good venue for selling books of all genres. Many potential customers come to book fairs just to look for kids books signed by the author. This usually entails a fee to enter.

6) Craft fairs may seem like a good venue for selling books by the author, but it often does not work out for selling. Much depends on the nature of the craft sale, indoor versus outdoor, and the types of crafts that will surround you. An author may feel out of place sitting between a jewelry booth and one that sells bird cages. People generally don't attend craft fairs in search of books.

7) Miscellaneous venues are up to the author's imagination and energy. I've known authors of children's books who did well selling in a pet store. Their books were about animals, and the pet stores loved advertising the author's scheduled appearance. Another author did readings in the children's clothing section of a department store. Local independent television stations are always looking for

interesting people to interview. Check them out and contact the station managers.

BEGIN WRITING

What are you waiting for? The only thing holding you back is *you*. If you've been through this book and have an idea of what you want to write, just get started. You can always fix it later. We live in amazing times of no more white-out, no more carbon paper, no more typewriter repairs. We can zip through a manuscript and make corrections a hundred times faster than did Mark Twain and Ernest Hemingway. If you have a story to tell, or you have data and helpful information to convey, and you can find the time in your schedule, there's no better time than the present.

No matter what you write, you will eventually see your name on the cover of a book, under the title you created, with your credits and reviewer comments added in, sitting on shelves in your local library or in the homes of your children and friends. And when you sign that first book, make sure you say "my first autographed book" on the title page. You never know. It may be worth millions one day.

Good luck.

SAMPLE MANUSCRIPT TEXT

THE UPSIDE TO MURDER

PROLOGUE

<u>July 19, 2011 – Delray Beach, Florida</u>

Like most hot summer Sundays at the beach, hoards of people frolicked about, swimming, walking, basking on lounges and blankets, while lifeguards flirted with young girls in string bikinis. Five-year-old Rusty Conroy loved playing in the sand, making castles, digging holes with his pail and shovel, wading in the surf, and showing his mommy all the new shells he found, including the ones that looked like a spinning top. The noon sun blazed overhead amid a cloudless sky, which made the sea water feel so refreshing.

Nearby, Mommy lay prone on a blanket as her new boyfriend rubbed lotion over her back. Rusty didn't like him very much because he only paid attention to his mother, not him. Besides, his grey hair made him look like an older man. Country music

sounded from a portable radio by a neighboring group. Two

teenage boys played Frisbee by the surf. Little Rusty suddenly felt

an urge to pee, but he knew better than to do anything without

permission, so he ran and asked his mommy, "I gotta go to the

bathroom? Can I go? Can I go?"

"What do you gotta do? Number one, or number two?" she

asked.

"Number one," Rusty replied, crossing his legs.

Mommy looked left and right, then motioned with her hand.

"It's okay, honey. There's no bathroom around here. Why don't

you just like, ya know, go in the water."

"Okay, Mommy."

At that, Rusty obeyed his mommy's orders, raced down to the

surf's edge and promptly yanked the bathing suit down to his

ankles, stood under the heavens and proudly peed, producing a

stream that shot at least three feet from his tiny body. He made

sure to stand in the water, just as he was told. A young woman nearby covered her mouth, laughing, then turned her daughter's eyes away. But it didn't faze Rusty.

Just as he was pulling up his suit, Rusty spotted a colorful object under the water, about six feet away, oscillating to the movement of the waves. He looked closer and saw it was red. It didn't seem to belong there. His mommy told him not to enter the deeper water without her presence, but this seemed shallow enough and the waves were not strong, so he looked closer. Then, closer. When he stepped to where the water came up to his chest, he heard his mother scream from behind, "Rusty, come back here! Get out of that water, now!"

But he was very close, so he leaned over and reached for the red item and fell in, face first. *Splash!* While underwater, he grabbed the object with both hands. Within seconds, he felt someone grab onto him, pulling him back toward the beach. It was his mommy's boyfriend who seemed mad. But Rusty still had his trophy.

SAMPLE SYNOPSIS

Suspense/Police thriller   81,100 words

THE UPSIDE TO MURDER

By Marshall Frank

SYNOPSIS

In *The Upside to Murder*, Miami-based physician, Dr. Orville T. Madison, activist and pillar of the community, stealthily lures two teens from the hood onto his boat at 10 p.m., under a ruse of unloading drugs. Miles out in the darkened Atlantic, he shuts off the engines, points his gun and demands the name of the third unknown suspect who had been involved in the rape/shooting of his daughter and her boyfriend four weeks earlier. Once he has the name, he kills them both and trolls their bodies for the sharks.

Though blinded in one eye, his sixteen-year-old Cassandra had survived the assault. Her boyfriend was killed.

Haunted by the memory of his sister's ordeal with the justice system twenty years before, which ended in her suicide, the esteemed African-American physician embarks on an obsessive mission to protect his traumatized daughter from the certain nightmare of criminal trials and vulgar accusations by eliminating the defendants. His attempts to track down and kill the third suspect before police can arrest him result in several amateurish blunders which ultimately lead the chief detective, Sgt. Ray Blocker, to his trail. The third suspect was wrongly identified.

A deep chasm forms within his family after they learn that Cassandra is pregnant. Already under psychiatric care and emotionally fragile, she and her mother demand termination of the pregnancy, while Orville stubbornly refuses for religious reasons. After a depressed Cassandra attempts suicide, Orville reluctantly capitulates and secretly flies his daughter to the Bahamas where he finds no one to perform the abortion, other than himself.

This highly charged story is immersed with subplots concerning forensic evidence, religious conflict, misidentification and the parallel problems of the senior detective who is dealing with many personal struggles of his own. Before his capture, facing a certain prison sentence, Doctor Madison pilots his plane into a nosedive to make it appear like an accident, leaving his wife and child with a double-indemnity life insurance payoff.

An epilogue provides closure concerning the plight of several sub-characters including the elder detective (Ray Blocker) who is admonished by the police department for falling in love with a call girl; Kyle Atkins, the rookie detective under the tutelage of Detective Blocker who struggles to impress his mentor; the innocent black man from the hood who flees South Florida to escape capture for a murder he did not commit; and Addie Madison who is left a widow and single mother in the wake of the ordeal.

www.marshallfrank.com

SAMPLE QUERY LETTER

Your Name
Address
City, State Zip
Phone
Email

15 October 2011

Ms. Jane Smith, Literary Agent
1234 Elm Street
Melbourne, FL 32901

Dear Ms. Smith:

I am a retired police captain/homicide detective from Miami-Dade Police with thirty years experience. I am a published author with eleven books in the marketplace, fiction and non-fiction. Five books were published by small press traditional publishers, and five were self-published.

In *The Upside to Murder* (suspense/police thriller), Miami-based Doctor Orville T. Madison, pillar of the community, lures two young men from the hood onto his boat at 10 p.m. under a ruse of unloading drugs. Once out in the darkened Atlantic, he shuts off the engines, points his gun and emotionally demands the name of a third subject that had been involved in the rape/shooting of his daughter four weeks earlier. He kills the youths and trolls their bodies for the sharks. His 16 year-old daughter had survived the vicious assault four weeks earlier.

The respected African-American physician embarks on an obsessive mission to protect his daughter from the ordeal of criminal trials and traumatic accusations. Thus, his quest to eliminate the future trial defendants. Attempts to track down the third suspect result in amateurish blunders that ultimately lead the chief detective, Sgt. Ray Blocker, to his trail.

This is a powerful story with social and justice messages conveyed to the reader. It contains subplots and issues concerning pregnancy, abortion, CSI investigations, religion, misidentification and parallel problems of the senior detective.

I am an energetic marketing person and a good public speaker at civic organizations, books stores, libraries and conferences. I would be happy to partner with a publisher that has confidence in my work.

This novel is slightly over 81,000 words. Visit my web page at www.marshallfrank.com.

Sincerely,

Marshall Frank

SAMPLE: AUTHOR'S BIO PAGE

ABOUT THE AUTHOR

Marshall Frank is a retired captain from the Miami-Dade Police Department where he served most of his thirty years in Homicide and/or CSI. After retiring, he worked another four years with a major security company before embarking on a writing career. In 1980, he was called to testify to a U.S. Senate subcommittee about violent crime in America.

Frank has authored eleven books; six suspense novels, three books of essays, a book of short stories and a memoir. He has also penned over one thousand articles and newspaper editorials which were published in *The Miami Herald, Broward Sun-Sentinel, Florida Today,* and the *Asheville Citizen-Times.* He maintains an online blog relevant to many current political and social issues.

Frank studied classical violin in childhood and went on to play part time with Florida symphonies, chamber groups and other musicians as an entertainer.

He holds a Bachelor's Degree in Criminal Justice from Florida International University.

He lives in Melbourne, Florida, with his wife, Suzanne, a sculpture artist.

Visit his web site at www.marshallfrank.com.

ABOUT THE AUTHOR

Marshall Frank is a retired captain from the Miami-Dade Police Department where he served most of his thirty years in Homicide and/or CSI.

Frank is the author of twelve books: six suspense novels, three non-fiction books of essays, a book of short stories, a memoir and one how-to book. He has also penned over one thousand articles and newspaper editorials. He maintains an online blog relevant to many current political and social issues.

A student of classical violin, Frank holds a Bachelor's Degree in Criminal Justice from Florida International University. He lives in Melbourne, Florida.

His books can be ordered from his web site at:
www.marshallfrank.com
E-mail: MLF283@aol.com

www.ingramcontent.com/pod-product-compliance
Lightning Source LLC
Chambersburg PA
CBHW072025040426
42447CB00009B/1730